SKILLS
OF
LIVING

A Complete Course in You and What You Can Do About Yourself

William L. Mikulas

UNIVERSITY
PRESS OF
AMERICA

LANHAM • NEW YORK • LONDON

Copyright © 1983 by
William L. Mikulas

University Press of America,™ Inc.

4720 Boston Way
Lanham, MD 20706

3 Henrietta Street
London WC2E 8LU England

Library of Congress Cataloging in Publication Data

Mikulas, William L.
    Skills of living.

    1. Life skills.   I. Title.
HQ2037.M54   1983   158'.1   83-10367
ISBN 0-8191-3340-X
ISBN 0-8191-3341-8 (pbk.)

for BENITA.

CONTENTS

1. ABOUT THIS BOOK 1

SECTION ONE: GENERAL APPROACH

2. BASIC STRATEGY 3
 Will power? 4, Understanding vs. action 4,
 Relax 5, Set up a program 6, Take small steps 7,
 Revise your program 8, Help from others 8,
 Summary 9.

3. KNOW YOURSELF 11
 Written records 12, When and where? 14, What
 do you do? 15, What happens? 15, What you will
 find 15, Goals 16.

SECTION TWO: GENERAL TECHNIQUES

4. INTRODUCTION TO SECTION TWO 17

5. CHANGE OF SCENE 19
 Remove 19, Avoid 20, Restrict 20, Reminders 21,
 The big change 22, Social support 22.

6. RELAXING BODY AND MIND 25
 Relaxation area and time 26, Diaphragm breathing 27, Deep breathing 28, Muscle relaxation 28,
 Muscle relaxation list 31, Muscle relaxation
 practice 32, Meditation 33, Suggested reading 38.

7. CALM AND RELAXED LIVING 39
 Practice in relaxation area 39, Into the
 world 41, Other aids 42, Sleeping problems 43,
 Suggested reading 45.

8. GETTING MOTIVATED 47
 Rewards 48, Types of rewards 49, Simple
 contracts 50, Complex contracts 51, Example 53.

9. GETTING ORGANIZED 57
 Memory aids 57, Lists 59, Priorities 60,
 Suggested Reading 61.

v

10. OUT OF HABIT   63
      Good habits 63, Bad habits 64, Nervous habits 64,
      Desires 66, Disrupt the sequence 67, Over-
      loading 68, Unpleasant associations 68,
      Suggested reading 70.

11. WHAT DO YOU THINK?   71
      Positive thinking 71, Basic principles 72,
      Changing your mind 72, Developing mental
      flexibility 73, Quieting the mind 73, Observ-
      ing thinking 73, Evaluating thoughts 74, Take
      action 7 6, Reducing undesired thoughts 7 6,
      Increasing desired thoughts 78, All together 8 0,
      Talking to yourself 8 0, Suggested reading 8 1.

12. MENTAL REHEARSAL   83
      Examples 84, Variations 85, Suggested reading 86.

13. NUTRITION AND EXERCISE   89
      Getting in touch 89, Nutrition 90, General
      nutrition principles 91, Weight loss 92,
      Exercise 92, General conditioning 93, Muscle
      tone and posture 93, Flexibility 94, Burning
      calories 94, Meditation 95, General exercise
      principles 95, Suggested reading 97.

SECTION THREE: SPECIAL PROBLEMS

14. INTRODUCTION TO SECTION THREE   99

15. FEARS   101
      Relax 102, Know your fear 102, Infrequent
      specific fears 104, Non-specific fears 105,
      Anxiety hierarchy 106, Sample hierarchies 107,
      Reducing your fears: imagination 108, Reducing
      your fears: real world 110, Additional 111,
      Suggested reading 111.

16. EATING AND WEIGHT CONTROL   113
      Observe your eating 114, Small steps 115,
      Setting up a program 115, Feelings 116,
      Thoughts 116, Remove and avoid 116, Restrict 117,
      Meals 118, Desires 120, Support from others 120,
      Social eating 121, Long term maintenance 121,
      Suggested reading 122.

17. SMOKING   123
      How did you begin? 123, But why continue 123,

A stop smoking program 124, Reasons to stop 124, Excuses 126, Observe your smoking 127, Feelings and thoughts 127, Remove, avoid, restrict 128, Make smoking a commotion 129, Make smoking less desirable 129, Alternatives for hands and mouth 129, Quitting 130, Staying a non-smoker 132, Suggested reading 133.

18. ALCOHOL   135
Do you have a drinking problem? 136, Reducing drinking 136, Reasons to decrease drinking 137, Observe your drinking 137, Related problems 138, Thoughts 139, Remove and avoid 139, Alterna-tives 139, Decreasing desires 140, Cutting down 140, Staying free 141, Suggested reading 142.

19. SEX   143
Uptightness 143, Inadequate education 144, Troublesome beliefs 145, Sexual develop-ment 147, Professional help? 148, Get the facts 148, Know yourself 149, Communication 150, Medical checkup 152, Anxiety 153, General principles 153, Specific dysfunctions 154, Sexual fantasies 159, Conclusion 163, Suggested reading 163.

20. LEARNING AND REMEMBERING   165
Memory aids 165, Attention 165, Association 166, Mental imagery 168, Memory sytems 169, Studying 169, SQ3R 171, Suggested reading 173.

SECTION FOUR: EFFECTIVE AND HAPPY LIVING

21. INTRODUCTION TO SECTION FOUR   175

22. PERSONAL FREEDOM   177
Becoming freer 177, Simple examples 178, Personal freedom 179, Suggested reading 181.

23. HAPPINESS   183
Sources of pleasure 183, Your happiness 183, Pleasure and happiness 184, What doesn't work 186, What does work 188, You are responsible 190, Becoming happier 190, Beyond happiness 191, Suggested reading 191.

vii

24. LOVE   193
     Unconditional acceptance 194, Love yourself
     unconditionally 194, Loving others 195,
     Aggression 196, Suggested reading 198.

25. INNER PEACE   199
     Your center 199, Quieting your mind 200,
     Opening your heart 201, Unconditional
     acceptance 201, Going with the flow 203,
     Being centered 204.

26. MINDFULNESS   205
     Meditation 205, General mindfulness 207,
     Mindfulness of behavior 209, Mindfulness
     of body 209, Mindfulness of perceptions 210,
     Mindfulness of feelings 211, Mindfulness of
     mind 212, The witness 213, Be mindful 214,
     Suggested reading 214.

27. COMMUNICATION   215
     Listening 215, Honesty 216, I versus you
     messages 218, Problem-solving 219,
     Suggested reading 219.

28. CHOOSING A COUNSELOR   221

FEEDBACK   225

TECHNICAL OVERVIEW   227

PREFACE

There are two different prefaces to this book. For the general reader the first chapter (About This Book) is the preface and you should start there (p. 1). For professionals (e.g. counselors, psychologists, college professors) I have included a second "preface" (Technical Overview) at the end of the book (p. 227).

For the content of this book I am indebted to numerous sources and disciplines. I have particularly learned from my major teachers: my students, clients, and workshop participants. In the preparation of the book I received major and significant help from my partner and best friend, Benita. She made numerous suggestions about style and content. She also typed all drafts of the book, a task that was often tedious. I also want to thank several friends who made comments on specific chapters: Rod Voss (chap. 13), Dave Redfering (19), Bryan Standley (22), and Jack Keller (28).

WLM
April 1983

CHAPTER ONE

ABOUT THIS BOOK

This is a book with a lot of <u>practical</u> information about how <u>you</u> can significantly alter your life in ways you consider desirable. It is a course in you: how you act, feel, and think, and what you can do to change any of it you wish to change.

The information in this book comes from many sources. Some of the procedures have been proven in rigorous psychological studies. Some of the approaches are widely used in clinics and self-improvement programs; and you could spend considerable money to learn them. Some of the techniques in this book have proven themselves over thousands of years, while others are quite new. This book contains information across a lot of areas. Therefore at different places in this book is valuable information that you can use and which will work for you.

There is nothing to believe in! This book appeals to your reason, not your beliefs. There is no philosophy or theory of people you must accept. There is no reference to magical forces. Rather, you will learn to observe and know <u>yourself</u> better. You will learn effective procedures to alter your life, procedures that make sense to you. You will test these procedures out yourself and find which work best for you. You will learn things about your life that you can apply in many ways.

I know the material in this book works. As a person I have applied much of this to my own life. As a college professor I teach and do research on these procedures. I watch my students change their own lives and the lives of others with what you are going to learn. And, as a person who runs numerous workshops and self-improvement programs for a wide range of different types of people, I have seen these ideas and procedures work and have learned much about how they work best.

Section 1 of the book is General Approach. Here you learn basic strategies to take control and responsibility for your life, the overall approach of the book, and how to observe and know yourself better.

Section 2 is General Techniques. Here you will

learn techniques and procedures you can use in many
ways to improve your life. You will learn such things
as how to relax your body and mind, how to overcome
anxiety and stress, how to get yourself motivated to
do what you want, how to change and organize your world
to improve what you are doing, how to think more clearly, and how to reduce unwanted desires.

It is important that you slowly read, understand,
and practice the procedures of the first two sections
before moving on to Section 3. This is because Section 3 is based on knowing and being able to use the
approaches of the first two sections.

Section 3 is Special Problems. Here you will
learn how to deal with a variety of problems, such as
reducing fears, stopping smoking, losing weight and
controlling overeating, improving studying and learning,
and working with some sexual problems. These are common problem areas, so most readers will probably find
a chapter or two here of particular interest. But I
would recommend you read through all of the chapters
of this section, even if they don't seem to be directly relevant to you. By reading these chapters you
will get mental exercise in thinking about behavior in
general and how what you have learned can be applied.
This then will help you understand yourself better and
will help you think of things that apply to your interests.

Section 4 of the book is Effective and Happy Living.
Here you will learn how to become more free, how to cultivate happiness and peace of mind, how to communicate,
and how to be more conscious of body, feelings, and
mind. Some of you may be tempted to start with this
section. But it would be best if you didn't. You will
profit more from Section 4 if you first complete the
first three sections.

Now let's get started.

CHAPTER TWO

BASIC STRATEGY

Your present life has been influenced by many things in the past, such as your family, schools, friends, health, economics, and a host of experiences and opportunities. Some of the things in your life that you may wish to change you may be able to trace to some past influences. Perhaps you would like to change something in your past. Perhaps you think about how things might be if only you had....

But the past is gone! You can not change the past. Although this is obvious, most people waste a lot of time thinking and worrying about the past and wishing the past were different than it is. The emphasis in this book is to let the past go and get on with what you can do in the present. What are you going to do NOW?

Don't worry about things you can no longer change. Don't waste time being bothered by whether or not someone else has had better luck, more opportunities, better health, or whatever. Don't think of yourself as a victim of the past; this is only true as long as you believe it. The question is always "What are you going to to do now?"

The next thing to fully realize is that you are the one who must change your life. Although other people and books like this can help and guide you, you are the one who must do with your life as you decide. You have the opportunity, beginning right now, to make your life more successful and happy, but you must take responsibility for it right now. No one else will or can do it for you. There are no magic words. This book will help you accomplish your goals, but you will be the one doing it. What are you going to do now?

Watch out for excuses. At many different times yet to come you will find yourself making excuses for why you can not do something. Perhaps you will tell yourself you are too old or too young, too dumb or too smart. Perhaps you will tell yourself you don't have enough will-power, motivation, energy, or time. Just remember that you can always find excuses. Your mind is currently set to give you reasons why you can't right now change your life in the ways you want. Learn

3

to watch for your excuses and not get taken in by them. If you stay with this book and avoid your excuses, you will be surprised how much you can do to change your own life.

WILL POWER?

Many people think that the key to changing their lives is will power, a sense of pushing oneself, forcing oneself over a barrier, or struggling with some conflict. But pushing oneself is not effective if you don't know the direction to push. Forcing oneself over a barrier is a waste of time and energy if there is a better way around the barrier. Thus will power and motivation are useful, but there are more important things. When you finish this book you will have more will power and motivation, but that is not the emphasis of the book.

Rather you will learn how to be more effective and skillful so that things will be easier to accomplish. Then if you need to exert your will, you will be more successful. Right now you are to some degree swimming upstream in the river of life. You are trying to solve some of your problems in ways which are hard and unpleasant. This book will help you learn how to "swim" better, where to enter the river, and how to use the currents to your advantage.

The will power you need for this book is based on developing your ability to get on with what you decide to do without excuses, delay, or laziness. What are you going to do now?

UNDERSTANDING VS. ACTION

Self-improvement involves two important steps: (a) knowing yourself and what you are doing, and (b) setting up a program or course of action to produce the changes you want.

The next chapter and parts of later chapters deal with ways you can learn more about yourself and how you think and act. Sometimes this knowledge is enough to cause you to act differently. For example, a person may learn he tends to be too critical with his children and decide to be more positive toward them. Or a person may become aware of how often she is twirling her hair in her fingers. Then as she becomes aware of when she is doing it, she does it less.

4

However, in most situations increased self-knowledge is not sufficient to solve the problem. Knowing what you are doing and what you would like to change does not mean you have the skills or means to make the change. A person may know he has a fear of heights. But knowing all about this fear and how he reacts to heights seldom helps reduce the anxiety. What he needs is a program to reduce fears. Similarly a person may realize she smokes too much. She may know why she smokes, when she smokes, and how she came to be a smoker. But this is usually not enough to help her reduce her smoking.

Thus the emphasis of this book is what you DO to produce the changes you want. You will learn ways to change your world and yourself in the ways you want. This will then lead to desirable changes in your attitudes and feelings about yourself. The emphasis is on action, not just understanding. What are you going to DO now?

Thus it is very important that you not just read this book. It is a workbook. It is a book with things for you to DO!

RELAX

Everybody needs to learn to relax more. In this book you will learn ways to relax your body, your mind, and your approach to living. Here I wish to emphasize the importance of relaxing your whole approach to self-improvement. In this book I am going to discuss ways to significantly alter your life. Thus these are things of great significance and importance. So the natural tendency is to become very serious and concerned about all this and feel the weight of the importance of what you are doing. But carrying this weight is unnecessary. This book will show you how to accomplish many of your goals, so -- relax.

The process of self-improvement should be taken seriously, but not in a heavy-handed manner. Relax. The process of self-improvement should be approached as being exciting, interesting, and amusing. Relax. Learn to have a good time with all of this. A good sense of humor is a valuable tool in your own work with yourself. Learn to see the humor in much of what you do, including those things you plan to change.

The more you learn to relax, the more effective

you will be at whatever you do. Relaxing will help you see things more clearly and not get as caught up in some of life's traps.

Many people get upset because they see how far they are from goals they have for themselves. This causes them to feel bad about themselves and then they usually don't make much progress toward their goals. This, of course, is then accompanied by excuses about why they can't reach their goals, which adds to their feeling upset. All of this is unnecessary and undesirable.

If you have decided to accept responsibility for yourself and are about to start moving toward your goals, you are doing great. Relax. Accept yourself as you are right NOW and plan where you are going. The past is gone; don't be impatient for the future. Relax. Do your best and be content with doing your best. You are a good person. What are you going to do now?

SET UP A PROGRAM
The purpose of this book is to provide you with information to help you set up a program for yourself to accomplish what you want. Stop for a few minutes and make a list of goals for yourself: things you want to change in your personal life, interactions with others, vocation, or whatever. The table of contents of this book will suggest some goals.

After you have made the list, decide which of the goals you want to start work on right away. Don't try to do everything at once. Take things one at a time. Start with what's most important to you.

Now for each goal that you have decided to start working toward, write down some of the things you know you need to do on the way to the goal. Many of the things you need to do will be covered in this book. So hold on to these beginnings of your program and add to it and revise it as you slowly go through this book.

Some of the things you need to do are not covered in this book, things such as getting legal or medical aid, seeking out more education or vocational training, or getting a driver's license. Be sure to include such things in your program when appropriate.

6

TAKE SMALL STEPS

Sometimes the best approach to a problem is to take
it head-on. Some people find that the best way to stop
smoking is to one day totally quit. For some people
the best way to overcome a fear of public speaking is
to force themselves to stand up and talk before a group.
Such approaches often work, particularly if the problem
is not too serious. But sometimes these approaches
don't work, as with many people who can't suddenly quit
smoking. And sometimes these approaches make the person worse, as with a person with a fear of public speaking who makes himself even more anxious by forcing himself to speak to a group.

Thus an approach which usually works better and has
longer lasting results is to take small steps toward
your goal. A person who uses a crash diet to lose
weight may lose a lot of weight fast, but he will usually gain it back. And continuing the cycle of crash
diet, gain it back, crash diet is unhealthy. However,
the person who learns to control his eating and lose a
pound a week will produce better, longer-lasting weight
changes. Similarly a person who is out of condition
should not jump into a strenuous exercise program. It
is important to build up in small steps. If a person
has a fear of snakes, it probably would not be a good
program for that person to go out and try to let a
snake crawl over him. Rather, this book describes a
gradual way to overcome the snake fear without discomfort. Or a person who wishes to learn to meditate for
long periods of time should not try to begin with a
three hour meditation. Rather, it is better to start
with five or ten minutes and build up.

So look for ways of breaking down your goals into
a sequence of small steps. Many people never move
toward a goal because it seems too far away. But all
you have to do, and all you can do, is to get started
by taking a step in the direction of your goal. A
thousand mile journey begins with one step. Many
people have many large tasks or projects in their lives
that they will get to as soon as they have sufficient
time. But the time never seems to come and the project remains undone. A better approach is to break
the project into smaller components that can be done
in smaller amounts of time. Similarly, if you are
working on a large task, such as doing a thorough
house-cleaning after a large party, it will often be
less overwhelming and more pleasant if you focus your

attention on just a part at a time. Take a small piece, such as cleaning the kitchen table, focus on that and do it, and then move on to another part of the whole task.

Don't be a perfectionist or concerned with un-reasonable goals. Relax. Be concerned you are moving toward your goal; don't be concerned you have not yet reached your goal. Be patient. Remember that the effects of many changes, such as those that follow physical exercise or quieting your mind, are subtle at first and may take a few months before you are aware of the benefits. Take on one day at a time!

Also take this book in small steps. Do not just read it through. Read it slowly. Think about what you read and how it relates to you. Come up with examples from your life that relate to what is being discussed. Take notes, underline, write in the margins, or do whatever with this book to make it more useful and per-sonal to you. Test out the ideas in this book and see what works for you.

REVISE YOUR PROGRAM
The program you gradually set up for yourself will need to be continually revised and added to. You need to be flexible with your program as you learn new things and find those approaches that work best for you.

You will probably make mistakes on the way to your goals. This is okay; everyone makes mistakes. In fact, making mistakes is often the best way to learn. You may really mess up a couple of times. This is fine as long as you learn from it. What caused the problem? What will you do differently next time? When you make a mistake or mess up, don't complain or fall into ex-cuses or get stuck in things now past. What are you going to do now? Get on with it. Continue with your program and if necessary revise your program based on what you learned from your mistakes.

Everything in this book has been tested and proven with large numbers of people. You can make it work for you if you set up a program for yourself and revise it as you learn. Relax, take small steps, and be content as long as you make progress.

HELP FROM OTHERS
Although the emphasis of this book is on self-

improvement, it is often useful to enlist others to help you with your program. For example, people in your family who know you well can offer valuable advice and support for your program. Similarly, you may find that talking about your program with friends may help you clarify in your own mind what is really going on and what needs to be done.

It is also useful to exchange ideas and support with people who are working on similar problems as yours. You may wish to join or organize a group to discuss programs for specific problems, such as over-eating or smoking. Or you may wish to organize a group to discuss self-improvement in general. This book might be one book you all read, discuss, and add to.

You will be surprised at how much you will be able to change your life with your own programs. Many things that people pay a professional for, you can do for your-self. But for some problems for some people it is best to see a counselor or therapist for assistance. The last chapter, Choosing a Counselor, offers some advice on choosing such a helper. If you are using this book and go see a counselor, ask the counselor how this book interrelates with his approach.

If you have any physical limitations, be sure to check with your doctors or advisors before doing any-thing physical, such as physical exercises or body relaxation exercises.

Finally, at the end of most chapters I list some suggested readings for those of you who want or need to go into some areas in greater detail. If any of these books are not available in your library or bookstore, you can order them through many bookstores or directly from the publisher (most bookstores have publishers' addresses).

SUMMARY
You need to help yourself. What are YOU going to do now?
Understanding a problem is seldom enough. What are you going to DO now?
The past is gone. What are you going to do NOW?
Set up a program. Relax. Take small steps. Re-lax. Revise your program. Relax.

CHAPTER THREE

KNOW YOURSELF

The necessary first step toward self-improvement is getting to know yourself better. It is important to become a better observer of yourself, seeing more objectively exactly what you do and when you do it.

Your mind, like everyone's mind, distorts things away from reality and toward the way you wish things to be. Everybody, to varying degrees, misperceives things about himself and the world. This is the natural way the human mind works. Thus a person who smokes might believe he smokes fewer cigarettes than he actually does smoke. Or a person who considers herself to be a loving person might perceive herself to be more loving than she actually is, misperceiving some situations in which she is not acting in a loving manner. Or a businessman, who believes his co-workers are plotting against him, might misperceive things his co-workers say.

Everybody's mind works this way to some degree. So it is perfectly natural if your mind misperceives in some situations. If a person misperceives too much, he may need professional help. The rest of us need to cut back on our misperceptions and know ourselves better.

The first step is to practice being honest with yourself. Try to see yourself and the world as they are, not how they should be or how you want them to be. Come to grips with what is now. Learning to be honest with yourself is much harder than it sounds. But it is readily mastered by patiently taking small steps. Continually try to be more and more honest with yourself. Look for ways you misperceive things to fit your beliefs and desires.

Remember that misperceiving makes you less effective and causes problems in your dealing with yourself, other people, and the world. If you misperceive how much you drink, you may not realize you have a drinking problem. If you misperceive how people act toward you, you may end up in unnecessary conflicts.

Make friends with yourself. See yourself objectively. Accept and love yourself as you are, not how

you should be or how you will be. If there are aspects
of your life that need improvement, accept and love
yourself as a person who needs some improvement, and
then do something about it. But don't close your eyes
to your needs or be unaccepting of yourself because
of these needs. As long as you are doing your best
and progressing toward your goals, you should accept
yourself as you are now. Relax and accept yourself.
Relax and love yourself. Make friends with yourself.
You are always with you, so be sure you are a good friend
to yourself.

If you are not a friend of yourself, you add a lot
of unnecessary anxiety and unhappiness to your life.
Note that you are now totally responsible for this.
Throughout this book you will learn many ways to help
you like yourself more and become more and more happy.
If you do not accept yourself as you are, you will misperceive and overlook things that are important to your
goals. Consider a woman who does not like the way her
hair looks. The anxiety she feels toward her hair has
a number of bad side effects including the following:
(1) the anxiety impairs her learning about her hair
and what she can best do with it; (2) the anxiety impairs her thinking about her hair and different things
she might try; and (3) the anxiety impairs her perceptions of what people really think about her hair. Thus
the woman's feeling anxious about her hair impairs her
solving the problem and adds more anxiety. She would
do much better if she would decide to improve her hair
as a goal, relax, and accept herself as she is.

The reasoning applied to the hair problem above
could be applied to most problems. Stop and think about
how one or two of your problems or goals relate to what
has been said so far. Really stop and do this!

WRITTEN RECORDS

The use of written records is one of the best
ways to learn more about yourself and cultivate observing yourself more objectively. By writing things down
you rely less on your memory, which is often a source
of misperception. By writing things down you can more
easily see some common patterns. Thus the use of written records is a valuable way to learn more about yourself, whether it be the way you act or feel or think.

One way of keeping written records is with a small
notebook you carry with you, as in your pocket or purse.

Here you can keep records, as will be described below, of things as they happen during the day. If you are concerned about how often you get angry or have a drink, then each time one of these happens you can record it in your notebook. These records will provide useful information for changing what you want to change.

Another type of record is a log or diary in which you make daily entries related to your problems, goals, or interests. If you are a very anxious person, near the end of each day you might make a list of those situations that made you anxious and how you handled them. If you are interested in your dreams, you should keep a dream diary by your bed and whenever you wake up, immediately record your dreams in it. If you are working on your own personal or spiritual development, you might keep a daily diary of what you learn each day, what you consider important, and suggestions you have for yourself.

When practical, the notebook is better than the diary, for the notebook gets you to record fairly soon after the event, while the diary requires you to remember what happened until later.

When keeping records it is very useful to count as much as possible: count how many cigarettes you actually smoke each day, count how many times you bite your fingernails each day, or count how many times you speak critically to others. Counting helps in many ways. Counting forces you to see just how much you really do something. This helps you be honest with yourself. This can also be motivating. For example, a man may find by counting that he twirls his mustache much more than he thought. This finding then motivates him to change that habit. Counting also helps you keep track of where you are so you can watch your progress and take the right sequence of small steps. Counting may be a little work, but it will be worth it.

Your notebook is a good device for counting, for every time you do what you are counting, such as smoking a cigarette, you can make a mark in your notebook. Another good device for counting is a wristcounter, such as are used by some golfers. This device is worn like a wristwatch; and every time you do what you are counting, you push a lever which adds to your count.

Get in the practice of counting whatever interests

13

you. Count things you wish to decrease; count things you wish to increase. The mere act of counting will help you become more aware of whatever you are counting. And this increased awareness is usually worth the counting, for increased awareness (know yourself) is the first step to self-control. Take your daily counts and put them on a graph or chart which you put up in a very visible place. This graph will then show how your counts change from day to day and thus provide more information for your program.

Some things may be very difficult to count because they occur too frequently, such as nervous hand movements, or because they flow together, such as negative thoughts. In these cases you can count periods of time in which the behavior occurred or did not. Thus if you are concerned about how often you think negatively about yourself, you may wish to keep track of half hour time periods, recording whether or not you thought negatively during each time period.

Counting is important information to keep in your written records. There are three other types of information you should keep track of in your records: When and Where, What Do You Do, and What Happens.

WHEN AND WHERE?
For this category you should write down the situations in which the behavior you are watching occurs. This includes the place where you are and what people are around. It should also include anything other people do and say that might lead to the behavior being observed. And it should also include any of your own thoughts and feelings that might cue the behavior.

A person who is recording his smoking might record under "when and where" that he smokes when he feels tense, when he has a drink, when he is in social gatherings, and after dinner. An overweight person might record eating when watching TV, fixing meals, and feeling nervous. A person might record feeling anxious when people are looking at him and when in high places. A person who experiences too much anger might record exactly what people say and do that gets him angry. And a person who spends too much money might record where money is spent, how much was spent, who was with him, what emotions he felt before spending, and whether what was bought was necessary or a luxury.

This when and where information will be very use-

14

ful later on when setting up a program. After collecting this information for a week or two, you want to look for patterns and common elements. That is, you want to look for those situations or parts of situations that seem to be most responsible for cueing the behavior. For example, you may find that it is usually when you feel tense that you smoke, or it is when you are unsure of yourself that you get angry. If you keep good records, you will probably learn things about yourself that you did not know.

WHAT DO YOU DO?

For this category you should write down exactly what you do in the above situations. That is, here you are taking the behavior you are observing and writing down exactly how you act. Be as specific and exact as you can. The behavior might be fairly simple, such as smoking a cigarette or feeling anxious. It might be more complex, such as how you act with another person. It might be what you think, such as the things you say to yourself. Or it might be a combination of such things.

WHAT HAPPENS?

The last category of information you should record is what happens as a result of the behavior you are observing. What happens to you? What happens to others? For example, you might record that when you smoke or drink it reduces feelings of tension or anxiety. Or if you are observing feeling depressed, you might record that when you act depressed, family members give you extra attention. Again, this information will be very useful later when setting up a program.

A thing to keep in mind is that most behaviors serve some purpose or function. Most behaviors occur because of what happens when they occur. This is even true of some undesirable behaviors that might occur because of the resulting attention or sympathy from others.

WHAT YOU WILL FIND

From your records you will find out more about yourself. Also this information will be useful in your setting up a program for yourself. For example, if you want to lose weight and find you often eat doughnuts when you pass the doughnut shop, then you may want to avoid the doughnut shop until you get your eating under control. Or if you find that you primarily smoke

15

to reduce tension, then a major part of your program to stop smoking should include learning how to reduce tension, as will be explained later. If you drink too much and find it is largely due to social approval and encouragement, then you might wish to spend less time with certain people, or get your friends to support your drinking less, or learn to be less influenced by others when it comes to drinking.

Because of the importance to your program of these written records, it is usually best to keep such records for a couple of weeks before you set up any change program. Therefore it would be a very good idea for you to start keeping records now as you slowly continue in this book.

Even after you begin your change program it is useful to continue to keep records, for these records will provide further useful information and will also help you continually evaluate how your change program is working.

GOALS

After you have collected your written records, it is time to think more about your goals, where you are headed. Consider your general goals, such as those you listed when reading the last chapter. Be sure your goals are reasonable, something you can actually achieve in a reasonable time. Remember our strategy of taking small steps. If your goal is quite complex or difficult, break it down into a sequence of small steps. Be sure your goal and the steps leading to it are objective. That is, it should be very clear when you have reached the goal in terms of what you can do. Thus a goal of "losing weight" is not as useful as a plan to lose one pound per week until you reach a weight of 126. Or a plan to be "more friendly" is not as useful as a goal that is stated in terms of smiling more or starting conversations with new people. All your goals and programs should be as specific as possible in terms of what you will do.

After keeping records and deciding on goals, it is now time to work out a program for reaching your goals. And that is what the rest of this book is about. As you go through this book,note different things that might be part of your program. Experiment to find what works well for you. Then gradually develop a program which will help you achieve whatever you want.

CHAPTER FOUR

INTRODUCTION TO SECTION TWO

The chapters of this section will provide you with techniques and tools that you can use in many ways for your own self-improvement and personal growth. Be sure you have carefully read the last two chapters before continuing on to this section.

Although some of the chapters in this section will be of more interest and use to you than others, it will probably be to your advantage to go through all the chapters. Take your time and slowly read each chapter thinking about how it applies to your life, your problems, and your goals. But don't just read; remember this is a book of things to do. It is very important that you put into practice what you read about. And all this time you will learn more and more about yourself.

As you read the material in these chapters, experiment with it, find what works best for you. Then include what you are learning into your programs that lead toward your goals. For areas where you want to learn more, go to some of the suggested readings.

You are about to learn many powerful tools that will work for you. Let's go!

CHAPTER FIVE

CHANGE OF SCENE

Various situations cue off different behaviors in people. You can probably think of a place or setting in which you feel romantic. Also you can think of situations in which you feel relaxed. Similarly, there are many cues, such as particular pictures or certain smells and songs, that trigger off various emotions, memories, and thoughts in you.

The world continually presents cues to you that influence how you think, act, and feel. An important part of Know Yourself (Chapter 3) is to observe and learn about the cues that affect your life. After you have learned about them you can alter some of the cues as a help in influencing your own behavior. Thus if you wish to feel more romantic, you might light some candles or put on special music. If you wish to practice meditation, you might light some incense and wear a particular shirt.

Similarly, you will discover many cues that trigger off undesirable behaviors. By changing these cues you can reduce the undesirable behavior. Thus a useful strategy in decreasing or eliminating a behavior you don't want is to identify and change the cues or situations that tend to lead to the behavior. This may be all that you have to do. But in most cases you will need to do other things as well to reduce the bahavior, things discussed in later chapters. But changing the cues is usually a good first step. Later, after the behavior is under control, you won't have to worry about the cues as much; they will have less influence on you.

But at first, a change of cues or change of scene is an important step. There are three basic ways to do this: remove, avoid,and restrict.

REMOVE
After you have identified cues that trigger an undesired behavior, see if there are ways you can remove some of the cues from your world.

If smoking is a concern of yours, you may observe that having cigarettes in sight or ashtrays on the table

19

make it more likely that you will smoke. If this is
true, then remove all of these from sight. If you are
designing a program to reduce smoking, then one part of
the program should be to go through your home and office and remove from sight all cigarettes, ashtrays,
matches, lighters and so forth.

Similarly, if you wish to lose weight, then part of
your program should involve removing as many cues as
possible which trigger eating. This would involve
such things as taking the candy bowl off the table and
getting the snacks out of the car.

If spending too much money is a problem, then part
of what you might do is keep cash out of your pockets
or get rid of some or all of your credit cards.

When working on getting control of some of your
emotions, you may at first temporarily remove pictures
of people and situations that make you upset.

AVOID
Some of the cues for undesirable behaviors can't
be removed, but they can be avoided. When trying to
reduce smoking you might avoid cigarette machines and/
or the employee lounge. When trying to lose weight
you might avoid the candy store.

If excessive drinking is a problem, then part of
your program might be to avoid particular bars and/or
people where you tend to overdrink. Or when you are in
such a bar, avoid your usual seat and usual drinks.

If excessive spending is a concern, then perhaps
you should stay out of stores where you spend too much
or shop alone if you spend more when shopping with
others.

RESTRICT
Consider the person who eats too much. If he
keeps records of his eating, he will probably find
that he eats in many situations, such as watching TV
or reading. Now what happens in these situations becomes associated with eating. So now when he is watching TV, that situation cues the tendency to eat. So
an important part of controlling overeating is to reduce the number of situations that cue eating. The
best way to do that is to restrict eating to one place.

Thus as part of a program to reduce eating, it would be wise to restrict all eating to one area, such as sitting at a particular table. Then restrict eating to specific times of day.

Similarly, the student who uses the same sofa for studying, napping, eating, and entertaining dates may find that when sitting on the sofa and trying to study her mind runs to many associations cued by that situation. It would be better to set up a study area in which she does nothing but study. This might involve a special table and chair or a special arrangement of the furniture.

If you are devising a program to reduce smoking, then look for ways to restrict the situations in which you smoke. For example, you might have a chair in the basement for smoking. Then if you have to smoke, you go sit in the chair and do nothing else while you smoke. For example, don't read while smoking.

If insomnia is a problem, then part of the solution is to restrict the bed to sleeping, and perhaps love making. But do not read, watch TV, or eat in bed. Then only go to bed when sleepy. And leave the bedroom if you find after about 10 minutes you are not falling asleep, perhaps because you are caught up in the day's problems. (Chapter 6, Relaxing Body and Mind, will have more to say on insomnia.)

REMINDERS
    When setting up any type of program for yourself, it is usually useful to put up a lot of signs and reminders about what you want to do. A sign on the refrigerator might warn against overeating. A list on the bathroom mirror might give the daily exercise program. A note attached to your cigarette pack might remind you to keep records of your smoking. A message in your purse or wallet might remind you of how you are trying to reduce spending. And a reminder in your daily calendar might tell you what you should do as part of your general self-improvement program.

    Pictures are often good reminders. Pictures of fat people on the refrigerator might discourage over-eating. Or pictures of thin people might encourage weight loss. Pictures of drunks or of you when drunk might remind you to reduce drinking. Or a picture of

something you want to buy might be an incentive for
your program to save more.

THE BIG CHANGE

Later on, after you have developed a complete program for yourself, there will come the time when you
are ready to make a big change in your life. (Chapter
8, Getting Motivated, discusses picking the right time.)
This will be the time to change your life in some way,
such as stopping smoking, becoming more assertive,
or reducing anxiety. When that time comes, it may be
helpful to change many things in your life as a way to
break old habits and get out of old ruts.

This might involve rearranging furniture, painting
a room, buying some new clothes, altering daily rou-
tines such as when you eat, or joining a new club.
Shake up your old life and get on with your new life.

SOCIAL SUPPORT

There are many social influences on our behavior.
People do many things for the approval of friends,
family, co-workers, and others. People are continually
supporting some things we do and disapproving of other
things. One reason some people eat too much is to
please a parent or spouse. A common reason many people
have a drink is to be sociable.

Thus an important part of your observing yourself
and keeping records on some of your behaviors is to
see what types of social support you receive and what
you receive it for. Then if you find you are getting
social support for doing things you don't want to do,
part of your program should consist of changing or
avoiding some of this social influence. If your spouse
rewards you for eating more than you want, see if you
can get your spouse to change and reward you for staying on a diet.

Get people, such as family and friends, to support
you in your change program. When you are ready to
begin your program, tell these people what you plan to
do and how they can help you. Then their support is on
your side. Also if you publicly commit yourself this
way, it is harder to back out of your program. If you
tell everyone you have a program to stop smoking in
three weeks, it will be harder for you to slip up and
smoke too much around these people.

When enlisting the support of others, be sure to emphasize to them the importance of their help. Ask them to support and praise your good work and progress, not criticize your mistakes. And go out of your way to reward and praise them for helping you.

Practice observing how you think, feel and act. Notice the influence of various cues and situations. Notice the influence of social support. Think about how you will incorporate this into your change program.

CHAPTER SIX

RELAXING BODY AND MIND

You continually encounter many things in the world that can make you feel anxious, uptight, or off-balance. These include interactions with people, personal problems, difficulties at work, and many other situations. Similarly, you are exposed to many sources of stress from such things as the responsibilities of raising children, keeping up a house, demanding work, the great amount of social change, and general high pressure living in a fast-paced world. In fact stress usually results from any significant change in your life, whether the change is positive or negative. Thus stress may come from getting a new job, being fired, getting married, getting divorced, taking a trip or moving, death of a friend or family member, change of life-style, and illness or injury.

Stress and anxiety, particularly when excessive, have widespread effects on the body. They produce a general weakening of the body so that you probably won't live as long and are more susceptible to many diseases such as the common cold and some forms of cancer. Stress and anxiety can also cause and/or aggravate a multitude of specific problems including ulcers, high blood pressure, heart disease, headaches, menstrual disorders, asthma, arthritis flare-up, digestive problems, skin ailments, and colitis (inflammation of the large intestine). Whatever organ or system is somewhat weak will be affected by stress and anxiety. No wonder doctors often recommend that their patients relax more. Remember the word "disease" as "dis - ease."

In addition, stress and anxiety have great effects on the mind. They can cause you to feel uptight or unhappy and can lead to a wide variety of psychological disturbances. Stress and anxiety will impair your perceptions, your thinking, and your understanding. They also cause your mind to race, such that you can have trouble falling asleep, avoiding unwanted thoughts, or finding the best solution to a problem.

Thus it is very important that you be able to relax your body and mind. For most people this is the most important thing they can do for themselves. But very few people know how to relax. You generally don't learn how to relax in schools, although it would be good if you did. Vacations and holidays are not the answer because there aren't enough of them. Also vacations often increase stress because of all that a person does on the vacation. Many people, not knowing how to relax, resort to drugs such as alcohol, cigarettes, barbituates, and marijuana. Similarly, people with sleeping problems often turn to sleeping pills. But many sleeping pills if taken continually actually cause insomnia. America is a drug-oriented culture. Drug companies, many doctors, and many advertisements offer us drugs as a solution to our problems. But although they may be a help in some situations, they are seldom a solution. Thus as you learn how to relax you can phase out any drugs you use for relaxation.

This chapter will teach you well-proven ways to relax. But you must do it, not just read about it. Learning to relax is a skill that takes time and practice. You can do it if you are patient and stay with it. In a couple of weeks you will probably already notice improvements and benefits. Then, with more time and practice, you will earn even greater benefits.

The next chapter will show you how to use relaxation in your everyday life to reduce anxiety and stress. Later chapters will build on these two chapters. For example, chapter 15 will show you how to overcome specific fears, such as fear of flying or fear of public speaking. But first you must learn to relax.

There are many ways to relax. Some settings may relax you such as being in the woods, hearing certain music, soaking in the bathtub, or smelling incense. You might relax by some activity such as singing, reading, or exercising. You might learn some special technique to relax, such as self-hypnosis or imagining pleasant scenes. This chapter describes three of the best ways to relax: deep breathing, muscle-relaxation, and meditation.

RELAXATION AREA AND TIME
        Using principles of cue control from the last chapter, set up a specific relaxation area in which to practice relaxation. This could be a little-used room, such as a guest room or large closet, or a part of a room. Then set up specific cues that you associate with your relaxation practice, such as a chair that you only sit in when relaxing or special clothes, smells,

and lights. After a while when you set up these relaxation cues (for example, put on your relaxation robe
and light some incense), it will help get you in the
"mood" to relax.

Arrange it so you won't be distracted while practicing relaxation. Choose a time of day with few distractions, and do things such as take the phone off
the hook and put a "do not disturb" sign on the door.
It is a time to do nothing but relax. If your mind
tells you that you are "wasting time," this is a sign
of a mind that needs to relax!

Set up a regular schedule to practice relaxation;
consistency is very important. If possible, it is best
if you practice at the same time each day. It is good
if you can practice twice a day.

Be comfortable in your relaxation area. Remove
tight clothing. Remove glasses.

DIAPHRAGM BREATHING
How you breathe influences how relaxed you are.
Understand the important difference between chest breathing and diaphragm breathing. In chest breathing it is
primarily the action of the chest going in and out that
forces air in and out of the lungs. Breathing is usually shallow. The shoulders are often hunched over and
the abdomen is often sucked in. Chest breathing is common in emotional and threatening situations. Diaphragm
breathing is based primarily on the rising and falling
of the diaphragm, a partition of muscles and sinews
between your chest cavity and your stomach cavity.
Diaphragm breathing is deeper and slower than chest
breathing. With correct diaphragm breathing the abdomen
swells, the rib cage expands, and at the end of the in-
halation the upper chest expands. To check yourself,
stand and put your palms flat against your lower rib
cage with the middle fingers just touching. Inhale
deeply and see if your fingertips are forced apart.
With good deep breathing they will separate by an inch
or two. Diaphragm breathing is more relaxing than
chest breathing and is also healthier because it is
more effective at getting air in and out of the lungs.
Diaphragm breathing is a critical part of yoga.

Stop and experiment with chest and diaphragm breathing until you can clearly feel the difference. Which
type of breathing do you usually do? Practice being

aware of the type of breathing you are doing in different situations. If you do a lot of chest breathing, then switching to more diaphragm breathing will help you relax and breathe better.

DEEP BREATHING

Now let us turn to a specific deep breathing technique that helps relaxation. Be sure to <u>do</u> it <u>now</u>. Sit quietly, close your eyes, and focus your attention on your breathing. Use diaphragm breathing and breathe through your nose if possible. Gradually let your breathing become slower and deeper. Then inhale deeply to a count of 4, hold your breath for a count of 2, exhale to a count of 4, and then hold for a count of 2 before inhaling again. Exhale as slowly and completely as possible and let the inhale occur naturally. Keep your attention on your breathing and let yourself relax and feel calm. Stop reading now and do this for a while until you are deep breathing with a steady rhythm.

Practice deep breathing for a few days in your relaxation area. Practice 5 to 10 minutes each time, preferably twice a day. You may find it useful to repeat to yourself over and over the suggestion "calm and relaxed" while you deep breathe. One way is to say "calm and relaxed" instead of the counts of 2. After practicing in your relaxation area for a few days, practice deep breathing at other times and in other places, such as riding the bus, walking, and waiting in lines. Obviously you do not need to and should not close your eyes in all these situations.

The next step is to use deep breathing in practical situations. Practice noticing situations in which you start to feel stress or anxiety. When this occurs, focus your attention on your breath and do deep breathing. Sometimes this will be enough to relax you; sometimes it won't. But with practice there will be more and more times when it will be enough.

MUSCLE RELAXATION

Relaxing your muscles is one of the most effective ways to relax your body. And relaxing your body helps to relax your mind. Here you will learn a set of exercises to relax your muscles. At first it will take some time to do these exercises, about one half-hour a day. But after a couple of weeks you can do them in much less time, and then eventually you can relax just by willing it. Everyone can benefit from doing these exercises for a few weeks, even if now or later you have another way to relax, for these exercises will put you more in touch with your body and also give you a sense of what a relaxed body can or should feel like.

The exercises should be done in your relaxation area if possible. They are usually best done in a lounge chair with your feet on the floor. However, they can be done in other positions such as lying on the floor. It is usually not good to do them lying in bed since you will have a tendency to fall asleep. Do the exercises at least once a day, twice a day if possible. Take your time when doing the exercises. For many people it takes 30 to 45 minutes at this stage. Try not to fall asleep. If falling asleep is a concern, set a timer or alarm clock to wake you up when necessary.

In these exercises first you will tense a muscle very hard for 5 to 10 seconds and then relax the muscle for 20 to 30 seconds, releasing the tension as fast as possible. When tensing the muscle you should focus your attention on the feelings of tension. _Feel_ the tension! When relaxing the muscle you should focus your attention on the change from tension to relaxation. _Feel_ the tension flow out of the muscle. _Feel_ the change from tension to relaxation. _Feel_ the relaxation in the muscle. The information in this paragraph is the most important for the exercises. Be sure you know and practice it. This practice will put you more in touch with your body, help you identify earlier when you start to feel tense or anxious, and thus help you learn self-control over tension and anxiety.

Below is list of muscles to go through with this procedure. Use this list for a while, as it has been well tested. If you have any special physical limitations, such as a trick knee or spinal injury, be sure to check with your doctor before doing any of these exercises. If you have certain muscles that tend to get cramps, do not tense them as hard as other muscles. Feel free to spend extra time with those muscles of particular interest to you. For example, if you get tension headaches, spend some extra time with the muscles of the shoulders and neck. As you do these exercises you will become more and more aware of your body and muscles you wish to work with. For example, you may find out over time that as you worry you tense muscles in your stomach, or jaw or forehead. Then you would want to do extra work with these muscles, which

29

then helps you worry less. Eventually you may even de-
vise whole sets of special exercises for yourself. The
suggested readings may help here.

Sometimes when you relax your body you may experience unusual body feelings such as muscle twitches
or the sensation of floating. These are common and
nothing to worry about. Just let the feelings go,
notice them, and continue to relax. Remember in doing
these exercises you are always in control! For a few
people, doing these exercises makes them more aroused
rather than more relaxed. If this happens to you, decrease how hard you tense the muscles. Gradually and
slowly tense until you feel the slightest increase in
tension; then stop tensing.

Now it is time to actually do the exercises. Go
to your relaxation area. Close your eyes and do some
deep breathing. Then begin muscle relaxation using
the muscle list below. Keep your eyes closed as much
as possible. Go through the list one muscle group at
a time, tensing very hard the muscles as described. (Alternative ways of tensing some of the muscles are given
in parentheses. You may wish to try these alternatives
later on.) Tense and relax each muscle group twice in
a row, tensing and relaxing as described above with
your attention on the feelings of tension and relaxation.
Each time after you have tensed and relaxed a muscle
group twice, relax and give yourself suggestions to feel
"heavy, calm and relaxed." Then move on to the next
muscle group on the list. Each time you see "deep
breathing"on the list, spend a couple of minutes doing
deep breathing. Let yourself relax even more with each
outbreath. Let each outbreath say "relax" to you.

When you complete the list stay quiet and relaxed
with your eyes closed. Then slowly count yourself
down from 1 to 5, letting yourself relax even more with
each count. Then stay relaxed for a few minutes. After
this, slowly count yourself back from 5 to 1 and slowly
open your eyes. Get up slowly and pay attention to all
your feelings. Remember you are always in control.

You may find it useful to have someone else or a
tape you make give you all the above instructions to
tense and relax, which muscles to tense, and when to
do deep breathing. This allows you to put full attention on your feelings without thinking about what to

do next. However, the counting from 1 to 5 and back to
1 you should always do yourself.

MUSCLE RELAXATION LIST
      The following is the list of muscle groups to be
tensed and relaxed. Alternative ways of tensing are
in parentheses.

   right hand: make a fist as if you were going to punch
      something (bend hand back at wrist)
   right bicep: bend elbow and "make a muscle" tighten-
      ing the large muscle in the upper part of the arm
      (press elbow against arm of chair)
   right arm: push arm straight out in front with fin-
      gers spread(reach for sky, or out to side, or
      back over head, or one after the other)
   left hand: same as right hand
   left bicep: same as right bicep
   left arm: same as right arm

   deep breathing

   forehead: wrinkle forehead and raise eyebrows (lower
      eyebrows and make exaggerated frown)
   eyes: close tight and wrinkle nose (open eyes as
      wide as possible)
   mouth: pucker lips and then frown, push tongue a-
      gainst roof of mouth (open mouth as wide as pos-
      sible or grin broadly)
   jaws: bite teeth together and pull back corners of
      mouth
   neck: rotate head in both directions (push chin
      against chest or head against back of chair)

   deep breathing

   shoulders: push shoulder blades back as if to touch,
      then shrug shoulders and pull head down into body
   back: arch lower back sticking out chest and stomach
      (do this after doing chest and stomach exercises)
   chest: take a deep breath, force out chest, hold
      breath
   stomach: tighten stomach muscles as if you were to
      be hit there (pull stomach in and/or push stomach
      out)

   deep breathing

   legs: (a) push against the floor, first heels and

31

then toes; or (b) with legs straight out, first
pull toes toward head and then push toes away from
head while turning the feet inward and curling
the toes

deep breathing

1 to 5 count
5 to 1 count

MUSCLE RELAXATION PRACTICE

You should do the above exercises for about 2 to
3 weeks. Then you can start to shorten the exercises
by combining muscle groups and tensing several groups
at once: both hands and arms together; forehead, eyes,
mouth, jaws, and neck together; shoulders, back, chest,
and stomach together; and then legs. Here you will
need to develop your own best way of combining the
muscle groups for tensing, the way that suits your
needs and interests. With the exception of combining
muscle groups, the rest of the practice should be
the same, including keeping your attention on the tension and relaxation and the use of deep breathing.

After you have done the above exercises with combined muscle groups for at least 2 to 3 weeks, you can
move to the next stage. Here you should practice going
through the list of muscles and relax them, but without
tensing them first. That is, you do everything the
same as at the beginning of these exercises but leave
out the tensing. Be sure to include giving yourself
relaxation suggestions such as "calm and relaxed"
while relaxing the muscles. Then every couple of days
do the exercises with tensing. Continue to practice
this until you can relax your muscles at will.

Finally practice relaxing combinations of muscles
without tensing them. Then move toward relaxing your
whole body at one time.

Some people find that it helps their relaxation if
they add the imagining of a relaxing scene. The imagined scene might be sitting on a sofa in front of a
fire on a cold winter night, lying on soft grass on
a warm spring day and looking at the clouds float by,
lying on the beach on a warm summer day, or lying in
a tent listening to a light rain. We now have four
components to help relaxation: muscle relaxation, deep
breathing, suggestions to self to relax, and imagining

32

relaxing scenes. Experiment with different combinations of these four until you find the combination that
works best for you.

As you learn to relax, practice relaxing at different times and in different situations. Practice
being aware of how relaxed your body is and then relaxing it more when needed. Practice being aware of your
breathing and use diaphragm breathing and deep breathing when needed.

After you have spent some time relaxing your body
(at least have gotten a good start), you can begin to
relax your mind with meditation.

MEDITATION
Meditation is a powerful way to relax your mind,
which also helps relax the body. As described here,
meditation is not a religious or occult practice. No
philosophy or particular beliefs are required. However,
if you are a Christian or Jew, meditation may help
you pray and listen to God. But here I am describing
meditation as a simple, yet very effective, way to
quiet and get control of your mind so you can use it
better.

Meditation will improve your perception and understanding of things, enchance your thinking and creativity, improve your concentration, and reduce the uncontrolled racing of your mind. Later in the book we will
build on what you learn here.

There are many forms of meditation. Here I will
describe one of the simplest, which is also one of
the best. Later you may wish to try other meditations
to find what works best for you; but it would be best
to stay with the one described below for a number of
months first. Instruction in meditation is offered
in many places including some community groups (e.g.,
some YMCA's), some churches, many universities, meditation retreats, and meditation organizations.

A special relaxation area or meditation area is
important. You need a place or setting in which you
do nothing but meditation. It might be a special area
in your house or a particular way you set things up
for meditation. For example, you might set up a special table with flowers next to a cushion or chair you
only sit on for meditation. These become associated

33

with meditation and eventually help cue you into that mood.

Wear loose and comfortable clothing. Do not meditate when you are sleepy, very hungry, or too full from eating.

The first step in meditation is to sit down. You can sit in a straight-backed chair with your legs uncrossed and feet on the floor. You can sit crossed-legged on the floor with a cushion under your behind. However you sit, two things are very important: you must be physically relaxed and your back must be fairly straight and vertical. Some people meditate better lying down, but for most people lying down makes it more likely they will fall asleep.

After you sit down, rotate around a little until you find a good firm position in which you are sitting straight, not leaning right or left or forward or back. Keep your head straight forward (nose in line with navel) and let it relax and drop forward somewhat. Keep your mouth lightly closed if possible. Rest your hands in your lap in whatever way is comfortable. One way is to put your hands on top of each other palms up, left hand on top of right (or right over left if you are left-handed), fingers on top of fingers, and tips of thumbs gently touching. Relax your abdomen. Use diaphragm breathing as much as possible. Breathe quietly and through the nose if possible. Close your eyes and keep them closed most of the time. Later you can experiment with meditating with eyes open.

After sitting down as described above, take a few deep breaths and let yourself relax as much as possible.

The next step is to focus your attention on your breathing. You can do this by focusing on the rising and falling of your diaphragm. Or you can focus on the feeling of air at the tip of your nose as it goes in and out. Try these two different ways and see which seems best for you. Then stay with that way for a while; don't continually switch back and forth.

What you need to do now is keep your attention on your breath, follow your breath. You may find it useful to say to yourself "in" when the breath comes in and "out" when it goes out, or "rising" when the diaphragm rises and "falling" when it falls. (When the diaphragm rises, the stomach usually goes in. And when the diaphragm falls, the stomach usually goes out.) Or it may be useful to count your breaths. Count each time you exhale and say "in" when you inhale. Count up to 4 or 10, and then start counting at one again. But just let your breathing go naturally by itself and follow your breath.

While you are trying to keep your attention on your breath, your mind will continually run off to various thoughts, memories, plans, evaluations, sensations, and so forth. The mind has been described as a drunken monkey running wildly from one thought or sensation to another. You will probably be surprised at how your drunken monkey runs about and how difficult he is to tame. But this is all natural and true for everybody at first. Through meditation you will tame the monkey.

So what you do is sit quietly and put your attention on following your breath. When your attention is pulled away by a thought or sensation, gently bring it back to your breath. Sometimes you will be lost in thought for a little while before you realize it. When you do realize it, return to your breath. Don't spend time thinking about how you were lost in thought. Just return to your breath. Sometimes you will fall into thinking about how well or poorly you think your meditation is going. As soon as you realize you are doing this, return to your breath. Each time you get pulled into remembering, planning, evaluating, or any other form of monkey business, gently return to following your breath. Don't try to stop thinking; just don't get caught up in thinking. When a thought occurs, just notice it and return to your breath. Don't evaluate or judge the thought; just notice it and return to your breath. Be very patient. Over time the thoughts will have less pull on you; you will get less lost in thought. This will improve your concentration and thinking. But you must be patient and practice meditation.

Similarly, many sensations will arise and pull your attention to them. You will hear various sounds, such as street noises. You will feel various feelings, such as itches. Treat sensations like thoughts. When you realize your attention has been pulled away by a sensation, gently return to following your breath.

35

When a sensation arises, just notice it and return to your breath. You will find that many sensations, including itches and pain, lose their power over you when you don't attend to them. But if you simply must scratch or move, go ahead and do it. Notice all the sensations that go with your scratching and moving and return to following your breath. You may encounter unusual sensations while meditating, such as colored lights or feelings of cobwebs on your body. None of these is important. No matter what sensation or thought arises, just notice it and return to your breath.

You will learn many things about yourself as you meditate, for as you quiet your mind things can get into your consciousness that are ordinarily kept out. This is an opportunity for great self-discovery. But during your meditation time don't think about what you discover. Just notice it and return to your breath. You can think about it later. You won't forget it if it's important. (If you really must, you can keep a notebook next to you during meditation to make notes. But this is not recommended.)

Although almost everyone can profit from meditation, a few people should not practice on their own. Some people can be overwhelmed by learning too much about themselves. Some people encounter too many negative things too quickly. Some people are too mentally fragile to meditate alone. So if meditation is unpleasant for you or you feel overwhelmed, stop meditating until you seek help from a competent meditation instructor or a psychologist familiar with this. On the other hand, meditation is not an escape from life or going into a trance. Meditation should bring you more fully into life. If you are using meditation as some type of escape, stop meditating. It is necessary to include this paragraph of warnings, but they really only apply to a few people.

Every meditator needs to watch for the tricks of the drunken monkey. He (or she) does not like to be tamed and will try to trick you out of meditating. One way he does this is by trying to keep you from following your breath by giving you things you "want" to attend to. If you want memories of the distant past, he might give you such memories. If you want personal insights, flashing lights, feelings of weightlessness, or whatever, he might give these to you just to distract you. Remember, no matter what he throws out to you, just notice it and return to your breath.

Another common monkey trick is to give you reasons why you should not meditate. Perhaps he will tell you that you are too young or too old. Or he might tell you that you are doing so poorly at it that you can't do it. One of his favorite reasons is that it is a waste of time; you could be doing something better instead. Since the monkey is your own mind, he will give you whatever reasons are the most convincing to you. If such reasons arise during meditation, just notice them and return to your breath. If they arise at other times, recognize them as monkey business.

When you meditate, just follow your breath. Don't try to accomplish something; just follow your breath. Don't evaluate how you are doing; just follow your breath. Relax. Accept yourself as you are. See things as they are. Being in a hurry or discontent with yourself or your meditation only slows down your progress. Relax. Follow your breath. Make friends with yourself as you are.

Start meditating for about 10 minutes and then gradually meditate for longer and longer. Experiment around and find the best times of day to meditate. Try to meditate at the same time each day if possible. Meditate twice a day if you can.

The effects of meditation are subtle and gradually build up over time. You must be patient. You will feel that you have good days and bad days, but in fact they are all of help to you in the long run. Stay with it. Gradually you will notice improvements in your meditation and then gradually you will notice benefits in your daily living. The effects are subtle at first but eventually become very powerful and significant. You will become aware of a greater clarity in your perception and thinking. You will find your mind more relaxed and open, but not gullible. You will find yourself cultivating a greater awareness and peace of mind.

When your meditation period is over, slowly open your eyes and then slowly get up. Try to be aware of all the sensations and thoughts that arise at this time.

After you have been practicing meditation in your

37

meditation area for a while, look for other times and places to meditate. You can meditate while riding the bus, waiting in an office, or sitting at the beach. Your breath is always there. Stop at different times during the day and quiet your mind. Practice paying attention to how quiet your mind is at different times. It will vary from very quiet to the monkey running wild. Eventually you will be very aware of your mind and when it is not working at its best. Then you can quiet it, tame the monkey, and use your mind to its full potential.

It is very important to periodically <u>carefully</u> reread all the above meditation instructions after you have started to meditate. Reread these instructions once a week during the first 6 weeks of meditation and then periodically after that.

This chapter has described several interrelated ways to relax body and mind: deep breathing, muscle relaxation, and meditation. This combination is extremely powerful and will yield great benefits from improved physical health to better mental capabilities. But you must <u>do</u> it. You must practice. You must have patience. You can't rush to learn to relax. The next chapter will show you how to use these relaxation skills, but first you must learn to relax.

SUGGESTED READINGS

The book edited by White and Fadiman briefly describes many different ways to relax and handle stress. The Rosen book is a step-by-step self-help program in muscle relaxation, similar to that described in this chapter. Bernstein and Borkovec's book on muscle relaxation is a brief, yet detailed, manual written for professionals, such as psychologists. The detailed descriptions will be helpful to some of you. LeShan's book is a good introduction to the nature of meditation and describes many different practices of meditation you can do.

White, J. & Fadiman, J. (editors) <u>Relax</u>. Confucian Press, 1976. Dell paperback, 1976.
Rosen, G. M. <u>The relaxation book</u>. Prentice-Hall, 1977.
Bernstein, D. A. & Borkovec, T. D. <u>Progressive relaxation training</u>. Research Press, 1973.
LeShan, L. <u>How to meditate</u>. Little, Brown, 1974. Bantam paperback, 1975.

CHAPTER SEVEN

CALM AND RELAXED LIVING

The previous chapter described several ways to relax. After you have spent a few weeks learning those
skills, you can continue with this chapter which shows
you how to have a calmer and more relaxed life.

Learning to be more relaxed in your everyday life
will bring you many benefits. You will enjoy life more
fully. You will get along with people easier. You
will think more clearly and understand better. You
will be more effective at making decisions and handling
conflict, and there are all the physiological and psychological benefits discussed in the previous chapter.

Becoming calmer and more relaxed does not mean losing your ability to feel emotions and react to things.
On the contrary, becoming more relaxed will make it
easier to fully experience the positive emotions such
as joy and love. Relaxation also gives you the skills
to better handle negative emotions and reduce or eliminate them if you wish.

Although anxiety may be useful in some cases, such
as danger situations, we are too anxious too often. We
often feel hurried, uptight, or off-balance. We need
to be more relaxed. This chapter and the previous
chapter discuss how to relax more. Chapter 15 discusses how to deal with specific fears.

PRACTICE IN RELAXATION AREA
In the last chapter you learned how to set up a
relaxation area and relax in it. Hopefully you have
been doing this for a while. It is important first
to learn to relax in a situation that does not cause
much anxiety or tension. Now it is time to learn how
to use relaxation as a tool to control or reduce anxiety, tension, and stress.

First go into your relaxation area and relax for
5 to 10 minutes. Then with eyes closed imagine being
in a real life situation that makes you feel slightly
uncomfortable. This could be a situation involving
another person; it could be a situation from work or
school. It must be a real situation from your life
which causes some, not a lot, anxiety or stress. Imag-

39

ine the situation as realistically as possible. Live the situation as if you were actually in it.

Pay careful attention to your body and your feelings of relaxation as you do all of this. Note changes in your body feelings as you imagine the uncomfortable scene. The changes may be very noticeable or fairly hard to detect at first. But they are there. Look for them. Going from being relaxed to imagining the uncomfortable scene may cause an increase in perspiration, an increase in heart rate, a tightening of the stomach, or general feelings of tension in different parts of the body. Learn to identify the feelings in your body that show you are becoming less relaxed and more anxious or tense.

If you have trouble doing this there are two solutions. First, try spending more time during your relaxation practice tuning into the feelings of your body. Second, use an imagined scene which causes more anxiety.

After learning your body signals, the next step is to practice re-relaxing yourself. What you do is go into your relaxation area, relax yourself, imagine an uncomfortable scene, and notice your body become less relaxed. Then stop imagining the scene, use your skills to relax yourself more, and notice the feelings in your body move toward more relaxed. Practice this set of steps over and over again with different imagined scenes of the same low anxiety. Keep practicing this until you can easily identify becoming less relaxed and easily turn the anxiety off and become more relaxed again.

Continue this practice using imagined scenes that produce more and more anxiety and tension. Start with situations that produce a small amount of discomfort and gradually work up to situations that cause a lot of discomfort. (About 15 to 20 scenes is a common number to go from low to high anxiety.) Stay with this practice until you can relax, imagine a very uncomfortable scene, notice the changes in your body, stop the anxiety and stress, and relax again. Remember our strategy of small steps. Take your time as you gradually imagine scenes that get more anxiety-producing. If you feel too uncomfortable imagining a scene, stop this scene and go back to a less uncomfortable scene. Then gradually work back up again.

What you are learning here is self-control of

anxiety, an extremely useful skill. It puts you in charge. In addition, the above training program can be applied to any emotion you want more control of, emotions such as anger or jealousy. To learn self-control of anger use the same set of steps above only use a sequence of imagined scenes related to anger rather than anxiety.

You will probably be surprised at how much the anxiety-control skills you learned with imagined scenes carry over to real life situations. You will find that being able to relax to an imagined situation of anxiety or stress will greatly help you relax when you encounter a similar real life situation. If you can control your anxiety or anger when imagining inter-acting with a particular offensive person, it will help you control your emotions when actually encountering the person. But to make your skills even stronger we now add some additional ways to bring your relaxation into the world.

INTO THE WORLD
Relax yourself before going out into the world. Then stay as relaxed as you can for as long as you can. The more you practice doing this, the better you will get. Also look for times and places during the day to practice relaxing. You might take a break from work to do some brief muscle relaxation or yoga exercises. You might use a bus ride to practice quieting your mind. You want to make a point of practicing relaxing several times a day in a number of different places and situations.

Next take the type of practice you did with imag-ined situations and apply it to real life situations. Practice being aware of body feelings that tell you that you are becoming anxious, tense, or whatever. Then practice stopping these feelings and becoming more relaxed. Some of the situations you encounter will only produce a small amount of discomfort that you can easily relax away. Good. Do it. Some situations will produce more discomfort that you can handle with some effort. Great. Do it. Working with these situations is often where you can produce some important benefits. Some situations will produce more discomfort than you can currently handle with your relaxation skills. Fine. Don't worry about these. You win some and you lose some. Just try to be as aware as you can during these times of your feelings and thoughts.

41

With time and practice your skills will get
stronger and you will gradually be able to handle more
and more situations that you could not previously
handle. With practice you will eventually be able
to handle any situation you want. You can be as relaxed as you want.

Learning these skills requires practice. But after a while you will have learned them well enough for
it all to happen automatically. That is, after sufficient training your body will automatically begin to
relax itself more than it did before. Your body and
mind will become more alert to sources of discomfort
and will deal with many of them without your needing
to be aware of it. You will become aware of more and
more subtle causes of discomfort that block you from
living most effectively and happily. And as you overcome these blocks your life will improve as you wish.
But first you must practice as described above.

OTHER AIDS
There are, of course, many other things you can
do to help have a calmer and more relaxed life. Here
are some further suggestions.

Generally try to take things easier. Don't take
yourself too seriously. Don't get caught up in your
own melodrama. Set an efficient, but not rushed,
pace for yourself. Take things on one at a time. See
Chapter 9 (Getting Organized) for how to assign priorities to the things you do.

Be sure to get enough physical exercise(see Chapter 13). It will help you feel better, sleep better,
and have more energy. Get outdoors regularly for
exercise,air, and sun.

Be sure you spend enough time on hobbies and recreation. Take many breaks from your work and your
ordinary day-by-day routine. Get away from your work,
house, children, or whatever. Get away for a week, a
weekend, or an afternoon. Get away often. Take retreats from your ordinary life, thoughts, and concerns.

Then, wherever you are and whatever you are doing,
try to relax more.

Get enough sleep, but not too much. If you have
trouble sleeping, then read the rest of the chapter.

SLEEPING PROBLEMS
     Many people have problems falling asleep and/or
sleeping well. Most such people can eliminate or reduce these problems with the procedures discussed below.
Therefore these approaches should generally be tried
first. Other people need other types of help for their
sleeping problems. Let us consider these cases next.

     Some people's sleep problems are caused by psy-
chological disturbances, such as emotional problems or
depression. Some of these people can reduce the psychological disturbances using parts of this book, while
others should seek professional psychological help.

     Drugs can often disrupt sleep. Excessive use of
alcohol, marijuana, or amphetamines often impairs sleep.
Continual use of some sleeping pills can disrupt sleep.
In these cases treatment needs to involve a decrease
in use of the drugs.

     A few people need professional help from a sleep
specialist. Such specialists can be found by referral
from your doctor or from a university medical school.
There is also a list of sleep disorder centers in the
suggested reading. The following are examples of
people who may need to see a sleep specialist: The person with excessive daytime sleepiness who takes frequent naps. The person who can not sleep and breathe
at the same time. This results in periods of non-
breathing (20-100 seconds) followed by gasps for air
and causes the person to be tired during the day. Or
the person who has constant body twitches while sleeping, particularly in the legs. Occasional twitches
are normal. But continual twitches are not and often
result in the bed clothes being all messed up and/or
frequent kicking of the bed partner.

     Some of these sleep problems are best detected by
having someone watch you for a few days while you sleep.
If necessary, see a professional. But most people can
improve their sleep as follows:

     Begin by keeping daily records in a sleep log.
Keep a week of records before beginning any change program. Then continue to keep daily records during your
program. Much of the information in the sleep log
should be written in the morning. Your log should
have these headings: pre-sleep activities, relaxation,
thoughts, and sleep times. Under the activities head-
ing, list all the activities you did during the evening

(such as after your last meal) before going to bed.
Under relaxation indicate how relaxed you were when
you went to bed. You might use a 5-point scale here
(1=not relaxed; 5=very relaxed). Under thoughts write
what you thought about in bed and what you said to
yourself about falling asleep. Finally, under sleep
times record approximately what time you went to bed,
what time you fell asleep, how many times you woke up,
what time you got up, and the total amount of sleep.

RESTRICT. The first step of the change program involves the technique of restrict, discussed in Chapter
5 (Change of Scene). This means that with the possible
exception of sex, the bed should only be used for
sleeping. Do not read, eat, watch TV, or do anything
else in bed. These other activities become associated
with the bed and keep you awake.

SCHEDULING. As much as possible get on a regular
sleep schedule, going to bed at about the same time and
getting up at the same time. Help your body learn a
regular schedule for sleep. Use an alarm to get up
at the same time each day. Do not nap much, or at all,
during the day. Watch your log to see how well you
stay on schedule.

RELAX. Put the day's work behind you before going
to bed. Finish what you can and then make lists or
reminders for the next day of things to do, consider,
or be concerned about. Then put all of this out of
your mind for the night.

Analyze your pre-sleep activities as recorded in
your log. Are you doing things that keep you from
relaxing? Are you doing too many things before sleep?
Are you doing things that are disturbing? Try to do
just a few relaxing things in the hours before going
to sleep. Just prior to going to bed, do some activity
that is particularly relaxing, such as taking a bath
or doing some pleasure reading.

When you get into bed relax your mind and body
using procedures such as those discussed in the previous chapter. Keep track of your success here in the
relaxation column of your log.

THOUGHTS. Watch your pre-sleep thoughts as recorded in your log. Practice quieting your mind using
the meditation skills of the last chapter. One way
would be to relax your body and at the same time quiet

44

your mind by focusing on the feelings of relaxation in the body.

If your mind is still upset by uncontrollable, unwanted thoughts, then see the section on "reducing undesired thoughts" in Chapter 11 (What Do You Think).

Finally, don't get caught in worrying about not falling asleep. This only makes things worse, for the more you worry the harder it will be to get to sleep, which gives you more to worry about, and so on. Stop these thoughts and worries. Relax your mind. Go to sleep.

SUGGESTED READING

This book is useful for people who have trouble sleeping. Some of the topics discussed are current sleep research, physical and mental relaxation, procedures to use to return to sleep when awakened, the sleep environment, reducing daytime stress, and a list of sleep disorder centers.

Coates, T. J. & Thoresen, C. E. How to sleep better: A drug-free program for overcoming insomnia. Prentice-Hall, 1977.

CHAPTER EIGHT

GETTING MOTIVATED

There are many ways you can improve your life, including ways suggested in this book. But if you don't do something about it, you won't make much progress. Therefore, you need to motivate yourself to do something now. It is very important that you make a firm commitment to yourself to begin a change program moving you toward your goals.

It is often hard to get started and/or remain on a change program. Perhaps people are telling you that you can't do it. Perhaps you think you are too old, too nervous, too weak-willed, too busy, too fat, too uneducated, or.... Forget all this and let's get on with making changes.

It is not enough merely to want to change; you must begin a change program. It is not enough to finally want to stop smoking cigarettes; you must choose to work at becoming a non-smoker. Wants go back and forth. It is the commitment to change that must stay consistent. You may waver. You may make progress sometimes and fall back sometimes. You will win some and lose some. And you may have to keep improving your change program. But you must stay committed until you reach your goals.

Make a list of reasons for change. Post this list and review it each day. Add and subtract to the list over time. If you plan to decrease nail-biting, possible reasons for change are being ashamed of people seeing your hands and having trouble picking up small things. Reasons to stop smoking might be related to health, money, odors, or addiction. Reasons for losing weight might include feeling better or looking sexier. Religious reasons might include giving up drinking alcohol for Jesus or giving up aggression as part of your Buddhist practice.

If you keep putting off doing something, make a list of reasons for doing it on one side of a piece of paper and a list for not doing it on the other side. You will probably find that the reasons for doing it are more important and more in number than the reasons for not doing it. The problem then is you are too caught up with one or two of the reasons for not doing and have let these influence you too much.

Choose to begin your change program when you are really ready to begin; but don't wait too long. You might begin your program on a day that is important to you, such as your birthday, the birthday of someone else, the beginning of Lent, or a holiday. You might begin on a day of beginning, such as the first of the month or the first day of spring. You might begin as a present to someone else, such as giving up smoking on your wedding anniversay as a gift to your spouse.

When you begin, make your commitment to change known to your family and friends. Get their help and support for your program. Review the section on "social support" in Chapter 5 (Change of Scene).

REWARDS
A useful and pleasant way to help you start and stay on your program is to reward yourself for doing it. Give yourself rewards along the way for staying with your program and doing what you should. Wouldn't you reward a friend for accomplishing something worthwhile? Aren't you one of your own best friends? (If not, you should be.) So reward yourself. For example, if you are trying to get into the habit of reading more, you might reward yourself by buying a small piece of clothing when you complete a particular book.

Now some people think they should stand up to their problems and overcome them with will-power, without any help or aids such as rewards. This approach may work with some people; but it is usually not very effective and usually not very pleasant. It is more pleasant to work on a difficult task when you sweeten it up with nice rewards for yourself. And the more pleasant you make it, the more you will enjoy doing it and the more effective you will be. Have a good time. The use of rewards can be a useful tool to help you change and learn new skills and behaviors. Eventually such rewards will no longer be needed and the changes in your life will be rewarding in themselves.

Another reason for rewarding yourself for what you want to do is that many of the rewards currently in your life may be working against you. For example, it may be more rewarding to eat a second piece of cake right away than not to eat it, even though the longer-term rewards of better health and appearance favor not eating it. So you reward yourself for staying on a weight control program that outlaws eating the second piece of cake. This continues until the long term rewards have a greater effect than the short term pleasure. Hence it is often useful to reward yourself for positive changes in order to offset rewards that are keeping you stuck.

TYPES OF REWARDS

There are many types of rewards and you need to determine which work best for you.

One type of reward is material things such as clothes, tools, records, books, sports equipment, and plants. It might be something you had planned to get anyway, but now you will require yourself to earn it. Or it might be something you would not ordinarily get, but it is a suitable reward for your accomplishment. The reward might be something that will help support the changes you make, such as clothes that only fit when you are smaller or a manicure set when you stop biting your fingernails. Or the rewards might be things you already own but now give to a friend to hold until you earn them back through your change program. For example, you might give a friend three sets of your favorite clothes and records to be earned back only by losing weight: one set back when you have lost 5 pounds, the second set back at 10 pounds, and the third back when you have reached your goal of 15 pounds lost.

Another type of reward is activities, things that you enjoy doing such as talking on the phone or reading a magazine. Activities are good rewards because they usually cost very little and because your life is filled with many such rewards every day. Practice identifying the rewarding activities that occur each day and start using them to reward yourself for doing other things. If on Saturday you plan to do yard work, which you don't like, and go jogging and ride your bike, which you do like, then require yourself to finish the yard work before you run or ride.

The following are some possible rewarding activities: reading, listening to music, phoning, napping, bathing, writing letters, knitting, cooking, looking at pictures, doing crossword puzzles, playing a musical instrument, practicing relaxation exercises, working on a hobby, playing with pets, gardening, working on a car, shopping, dancing, going to the movies, biking,

49

jogging, hiking, and playing sports.

A third type of reward is rewards from others. In addition to support and praise, someone else may want to do something for you if you progress on your program. This might be doing one of your household tasks for a week when you get your exercise program up to jogging for a mile. Or it might be washing and waxing your car when you have gone 3 months without a cigarette.

A fourth type of reward is points, which can be saved for other rewards. If you don't like to write letters but need to write a number of them, then reward yourself one point for each letter you write. Plan in advance what the points can be exchanged for,such as going to the movies when you get 10 points. The advantage of points as rewards is you can reward yourself all along the way for each part of your program. You can then have small rewards you can get for a small number of points and/or a large reward that requires a lot of points.

We have looked at a number of different types of rewards. What are good rewards for you? Stop and make a list of rewards that could be useful for you to accomplish what you want.

SIMPLE CONTRACTS
The way to use rewards is to make a contract with yourself, an agreement of what you must do in order to get the reward. The following are examples of simple contracts: After I iron five shirts I will reward myself by reading two chapters in my novel. When I complete my relaxation training for the day, I get to call my friend on the phone. First I will wash the dishes, then I will read the morning paper. If I practice the piano for half an hour, I may play solitaire for half an hour.

This type of contract, although very simple, is very powerful. One reason is that most people tend to do the opposite. They tend to do the rewarding things first and put off what they need to do. Or they do the rewarding activity first hoping it will put them in the mood to do the other. Thus a student might watch TV in order to get into the mood for studying. But this does not work. He should save the TV watching as a reward for completing studying.

As you get experienced at using contracts in the

right way, you will find many opportunities each day to
make simple contracts with yourself. Then the more you
use such contracts, the more efficient you will be; you
will get more done. You may also find that you feel
less guilty and enjoy your rewards more, for now when
you are having a reward you know you earned it and you
are not feeling guilty about things you are putting off.

Have a number of different rewards you can use.
Don't rely on one or two rewards over and over again.
You don't want to overuse and get tired of the same
reward. The more rewards you can choose from the better.

After you have been using simple contracts for a
while, you can move into the more complex contracts
described next.

COMPLEX CONTRACTS
Complex contracts are for projects and programs
you will be working on for a while, such as a long
range exercise program. These contracts specify exactly what you will require of yourself at each step along
the way and what you will reward yourself for doing it.
It is important that these contracts be written down so
you don't rely on your memory.

The first step is to specify exactly what you are
requiring of yourself. This includes what you should
do and what you should not do; but try to put the emphasis on what you should do. Be as exact as possible,
such as requiring yourself to lose one pound per week,
wash 4 windows each weekend, or do at least one half
hour of relaxation exercises each day. Don't just say
you want to study more. Be exact about the number of
minutes each day you will study. Don't put in your
contract you should write more letters. Be exact, such
as stating you will write at least 3 letters per week.

Remember our strategy of small steps. Have your
contract start with where you are and gradually build
up to where you want to be. If you want to write more
letters and are currently writing none, don't suddenly
require yourself to write ten letters in a week. Build
up slowly, such as requiring yourself to write one
letter the first week, two the second week, and so on
until you are writing four or more a week.

The next step is to specify what rewards you will
earn by fulfilling your contract. This should include
small rewards along the way as well as a few big rewards

51

for when you get to significant points. Thus you should have daily rewards for staying on your weight loss program and large rewards for when you reach certain weights. Or you might have weekly rewards for staying within your budget and a big reward if you do it for 3 months. Points are often good daily and weekly rewards.

Next you should write up your contract including all requirements and all rewards. Then post the contract in a very visible place, such as on the refrigerator door. This is a good time to tell others what you are doing and to ask for their help.

It is often useful to put up signs and notes to remind yourself of your contract and what you are trying to do. A sign on the refrigerator might remind you about overeating. Or a note in the bathroom may remind you to floss your teeth. Graphs are also very useful to give you a good picture of the progress you are making. Thus you might graph how many chapters of a text you read each day, how many times you bit your fingernails each day, or how much you weigh each day. Put the graph up where you will see it often. This will act as a reminder of your program and will also be rewarding as you see your progress.

When you have made a contract with yourself, stick to it. Be very careful to avoid exceptions to what you agreed to or excuses for why you didn't fulfill the contract. Once you start coming up with a lot of exceptions and excuses your contract will fall apart. Be firm with yourself. On the other hand, if you do mess up, be aware of what you did and how you can keep it from happening again. But don't dwell on blaming yourself.

The first time you make a complex contract it probably won't be the perfect contract. You might not be specific enough. You might not take small enough steps. The reward you choose might be too big or too small. Or there might be complications you did not think of or expect. Don't worry about this. Just redesign your contract and start again. With practice and experience you will become a good contract maker.

In some cases people can't come up with rewards that are strong enough to get them to do what they want to do or should do. In these cases you might want to set up a punishment contract. This would specify a punishment you agree you must get if you don't do what the contract says. The punishment might be doing some extra chores, giving away a favorite book or record, not going to a party, or not going bowling. You might give a friend checks made out to an organization you don't like. Then each time you don't fulfill the contract, the friend mails off one of the checks. You can also write a contract that contains both rewards for doing something and punishments for not doing it.

Making contracts with yourself, simple and complex contracts, is one of the most powerful things you can do for yourself. Sometimes this is all you need for your change program. For you know what to do and have the skills to do it, but you need the motivation to get on with it. Sometimes increasing motivation is necessary but not enough by itself. For example, if you want to lose weight you shouldn't just reward yourself for weight loss. You also want to change your eating habits, as described in Chapter 16.

This book tells you various things you can do for self-improvement. This chapter tells you how to get motivated to do these things. Thus you can reward yourself for record keeping, relaxation practice, organizing your life, working on nervous habits, or anything else. Start today using the ideas in this chapter. You can certainly be doing some simple contracting right away.

EXAMPLE
Susan was a 34-year old married woman with two children and an afternoon job. She realized she was not getting as much exercise as she should and her body had lost a lot of muscle tone. She also did not feel quite as good as when she used to be more physically active. In the last six months she had tried a few times to exercise more but was never motivated enough to keep at it. It was hard to get past the initial resistance. So she used some of the techniques of this chapter.

First she made a list of 9 reasons for getting more exercise, including "feel better," look better," "don't look pregnant," and "tenth anniversary is coming." Looking better and not looking pregnant was related to her need to tone up her stomach muscles, as with sit-ups. In a few months her tenth wedding anniversary was coming up and at that time she and her husband, Bob, were going to renew their vows, love, and plans for each other. Susan wanted to be in good physical and mental shape at this time. She posted her list of reasons on the door to her clothes closet and over time added more reasons to it. Each day she would read and think about one of the reasons on the list.

Susan began her exercise program on the day her children began school again in the Fall. She picked this time so she could be starting something new at the same time as her children. She also had more free time then and the weather was getting cooler, which she preferred for outside exercise.

In the past husband Bob was skeptical of her exercise programs because she seldom stayed with them. But this time she was determined and got Bob to help, encourage, and praise her, rather than discourage her.

Realizing the principle of starting where you are and taking small steps, Susan began her program easily. The first week she had to exercise on 3 different days, with each day consisting of walking one half mile and doing 5 sit-ups and 10 leg-lifts. The second week she had to do this on 4 days out of 7 and the third week on 5 days of 7. In later weeks she increased how far she walked and the number of sit-ups and leg-lifts. She also slowly added other exercises. For days when the weather was bad Susan had worked out how many minutes of jumping rope inside would substitute for the walking.

Susan thought a lot about her program and what rewards she would give herself for doing it. She then formalized the program and rewards into a contract which she wrote up and posted next to the bathroom mirror. According to the contract, on exercise days she had to do her exercises before reading the newspaper. She enjoyed leisurely sitting and reading the paper after her husband and children were gone for the day. Also each day she did her exercises she put a red X on a paper posted with her contract. When she got 10 X's she would get to buy a new record, but could only listen to one side. When she got 10 more X's, she could listen to the other side. Ten more and the first side of another record, and so on. Music was a very good reward for Susan and her program resulted in about two new records a month, which she could afford. Bob got involved and said that when she got to 50 total X's he would take her out to a dinner and movie of her choice.

To insure she did not slip, Susan also added a

potential punishment into the contract: If any week
(from the third week on) she did not exercise on at
least 5 different days (unless she was sick), she
would watch no television the next week. Susan did not
watch a lot of television, but enjoyed the national
news each day and her favorite science fiction series
where her heroes boldly went where no man had gone
before.

Over time she altered the contract as she changed
the exercise requirements. One time she made the mistake of adding in too many new exercises too fast. But
the whole program worked well. She never had to use
the punishment of missing television, although it came
close a couple of times when she thought she was too
busy for exercise. But she always managed to find the
time.

After about three months the exercising was part
of her life and easy to do. She no longer needed the
contract. She was feeling healthier, she looked good,
and she felt better about herself. These rewards kept
her exercising. As a result Bob started an exercise
program for himself. And on their 10th wedding anniversary they were both very pleased and excited about their
next decade together.

CHAPTER NINE

GETTING ORGANIZED

Getting organized means structuring your world, your time, and your tasks in such a way that you become more efficient and effective. It doesn't mean becoming compulsive about organization so that you lose time with all your organizing. It simply means finding an efficient way to do what you want to do.

Organization buys you freedom. As you become more efficient you will have more time to do other things, you will have less to remember, and you will become a more reliable person.

Each person needs to work out his or her own system of getting organized. Below are some suggestions.

MEMORY AIDS

A memory aid is a device to help you remember something, a reminder. It guarantees you won't forget something and so you can stop trying to remember it. One example is putting out clothes at night for the next day. Then in the morning, when you might be tired or rushed, you don't have to remember what you want or need to wear.

Car keys are a useful aid. If you want to remember to take something when you leave in the car, put it with your car keys.

Things out of place can catch your attention and act as reminders. A frypan on the floor can remind you there is a chicken cooking in the oven. An alarm clock upside down could remind you of something to be done first thing in the morning.

Notes to yourself are good memory aids. Notes can be put in pockets or taped where you are sure to see them. A note with a seldom-used appliance can remind you of some special way to handle the appliance. A note under your car keys can remind you of something to do when you leave in the car. Notes that require fairly immediate attention should be put in noticeable places such as on a mirror or on the refrigerator. Small magnets, which come in many forms and designs, are good for putting notes on the refrigerator and on the dash boards of some cars. Notes that deal with long term concerns, perhaps something to think about or something that won't happen for a while, should all be kept in one place. A small bulletin board is good for this. Finally, if you are going to be using a lot of notes, it is good to have note paper and pencils handy in many places. Thus it is useful to carry notebooks in places such as purse, briefcase, and the car's glove compartment.

Perhaps the best memory aid is a daily calendar with space for each day to write in daily events, special occasions, notes, and reminders. This can be, among other possibilities, a small calendar you carry in your pocket or purse, a bigger calendar that you keep at home and take to work, or a large wall calendar that hangs in the kitchen or study. In your calendar you can keep track of such things as appointments, social plans, and television specials. You can record birthdays, anniversaries, when the rent is due, when to change the furnace filter, or when to service the car. You can also include advance warnings, such as a two-week notice to buy a birthday present. You can put in reminders of things to do for your self-improvement program. You can include things you want to think about, check on, or worry about. This allows you to put these things out of your mind until it is time to consider them. For example, it may be that if you haven't heard from a particular person (or organization) in three weeks you need to contact him. Now, rather than think about this every day or so, put a note in your calendar for three weeks later and then you need not think or worry about it until then. You will find your daily calendar is a powerful organization tool that will become more and more useful as you learn how to incorporate into it more of the things of importance to you.

Another useful memory aid is a timer, such as a kitchen timer, which can be set to ring after a set number of minutes. The timer can tell you when food is done, when a show is on television, or when it is time to call someone. The advantage of a timer is that once you set it, you can forget about time and do something else. Thus if you need to leave home in 40 minutes, you can set the timer for when you want to leave or get ready to leave. Then you can do something else, such as read or listen to music, and totally immerse yourself in that activity. Similarly, you can eliminate unnecessary worry by setting a timer for when it is time to worry. For example, if you need or want to be

concerned if someone hasn't come home by a certain time,
then set the timer for that time and don't worry until
then. Thus the timer can be a useful tool for practicing being in the here and now, putting your full attention on what you are doing right now and not thinking
about the future until it is time to.

LISTS
        Making lists is a critical part of getting organ-
ized. It is a good way to help you remember things and
better organize your time. A list of projects to do
around the house helps you keep track of what needs to
be done. Also by looking at the list you might find
projects that can be combined or projects that require
your buying supplies at the same place. A list of books
you want to read helps you choose more effectively,
rather than just reading what is most recent or what
comes to mind. Most grocery shoppers use a list. But
you can also have a general "buy" list for other things.
Then when you are going shopping you can look at or
take your buy list. Similarly, if you don't go downtown very often, you might keep a "downtown" list of
things to do when you go downtown. Such lists should
be kept in one or two central places; you don't want
to misplace lists. A bulletin board is a good place
for some lists. If you have a lot of lists, you may
want to have a list of your lists.

        Other possibilities for lists include the follow-
ing: things in storage boxes or cabinets, things in a
safety deposit box, various service people such as house
or appliance repair, presents given to people, gift
ideas, and meals served to people. Some lists, such
as a buy list, are temporary, while other lists are
more permanent. For example, you might have a permanent "travel" list which contains things you might
want to do in preparation for a vacation and things
to consider taking. This list could be continually
added to and altered over time. After a while you will
have a list to consult before traveling which will
save you considerable time.

        Three-by-five cards are useful organizers because
you can make or buy (as in an office supply store) a
box for them. You can also make or buy alphabetical
dividers. Such a box of cards is useful for keeping
and filing recipes that are written and/or taped on
the cards under general categories such as desserts
and appetizers. Another box of 3x5 cards might be for
people, alphabetically by last name. A person card

could have the person's name, address, phone number, birthday, age, or anything else you want to know. A 3x5 card box is also very good for keeping permanent lists, such as those mentioned above. Such lists are filed alphabetically by their headings (for example: Travel, Safety Deposit Box) with a card in the front listing all the headings.

PRIORITIES
Nothing is more important in getting organized than learning to assign priorities. You can not do everything you want to do!! Stop and think about the significance of that. Of all the many things you can spend your time on, you can only do some of them. Therefore you must choose those most important to you. You must choose to do some things over others. The ineffective person chooses things based on current moods or what is most recent. The effective person works from a set of priorities.

Assign priorities to things on your lists. For example, on your "project" list mark the projects high (H), medium (M), or low (L) priority. Then primarily do the high priority projects first. If there is a medium or low priority project you would enjoy or prefer doing, then do a high priority project first and reward yourself by doing the preferred project next.

If the list is one you are keeping for a while, then periodically check your priorities. After a while a low priority item might become high priority, or a medium might become low. If you keep a priority list for a while, one of the things you will probably find is that many low priority items will lose importance or take care of themselves. What a time-saver, to end up not needing to do something that without priorities you might have done!

Schedule your time during the day to fit your priorities. Remember Parkinson's Law: Work expands to fill the time available for its completion. If you don't have some structure or schedule to your time, you may be spending much more time on various tasks than is really necessary. You may be wasting time. If you are not doing things that are important to you, you are not assigning priorities to your time. Schedule your time according to your priorities. Schedule time for such things as work, recreation, relaxation and meditation, or whatever. Use your daily calendar for your scheduling.

If you are spending too much money or somehow don't have money for what you want, you need priorities for your spending. Keep track of what you spend and what you earn. Then work out a budget that assigns priorities for money. Decide how much money you need and want to spend on such things as mortgage or rent payments, insurance, food and drink, clothes, and recreation.

You can't do everything you want. You can't buy everything you want. You probably can't go everywhere you want. You probably can't read or learn everything you want. You must choose; and choosing by priorities helps you get and accomplish what is important to you.

SUGGESTED READING

Winston's book contains many helpful suggestions for organizing in home and office, with emphasis on the home. Topics include managing time, setting up a work area, handling paperwork, managing money, using space and supplies well, and getting help from your children.

Lakein has written a very readable and useful book on getting organized, including such topics as setting goals and priorities and organizing and using time well. The book is somewhat geared toward business people, but there is useful information for everyone.

Winston, S. Getting organized. Norton, 1978. Warner Book paperback, 1979.

Lakein, A. How to get control of your time and your life. Wyden, 1973. Signet paperback, 1974.

61

CHAPTER TEN

OUT OF HABIT

A habit is something we do automatically, with little or no thought. In many cases we are not even aware when the habit is occurring. A "good" habit is one that we wish to encourage. A "bad" habit is one we wish to decrease or eliminate.

GOOD HABITS

Cultivating good habits is usually fairly easy to do and can pay high rewards. For once something is made into a habit it is usually easier to do; and once it becomes automatic you do not have to think about it as much. For example, you might realize it is good to floss your teeth daily. But you find that it is somewhat of a chore that you aren't really good at. So you only do it occasionally. But this keeps it a chore and you feel somewhat guilty for not doing it more. It soon becomes more and more unpleasant and so you do it very seldom. By now you may have come up with some reasons for why it is not as important as you once thought.

But it is different if you make it a habit. First you experiment and find the time of day you most prefer to floss. Then you require yourself to do it every day at this time. Soon it becomes a habit that is easy to do. The daily practice makes you good at doing it and any unpleasant associations gradually drop away. Now it is just something that you do.

The key to developing a habit is to be consistent, to do it every time. If you want to develop the habit of wearing seat belts in your car, then wear them every time you are in the car. This will make it an easy habit and lead to your being quickly aware if you forget. Also beware of excuses for not doing. If it takes a little bit of work or is somewhat unpleasant to get the habit started, your mind will come up with excuses for not doing it. Be wary of these excuses. You might tell yourself it is too much trouble to put on your seat belt for the few blocks you will ride to the store. But it is bad practice to give in to such thinking. And in this case the reasoning is false: You need your seat belt for short rides, since this is when many accidents occur that can be reduced with seat belts.

For more complex things you can develop whole habitual rituals. For example, you might have a house check ritual, a sequence of things you want to check in your house before leaving it. This might include where the pets are, whether the coffee maker is off, and whether the doors and windows are closed. Making it a habit consists of having a set sequence of steps of checking that you go through in a set order every time you leave the house. Once it becomes a habit it can be done quickly with little thought, thus saving you time. Also later on you don't have to try to remember if you checked something (Did I leave the oven on?) because you know it was part of your ritual, thus saving you worry.

BAD HABITS

On the other hand there are many undesirable things we do out of habit, such as biting fingernails or automatically lighting up a cigarette after dinner. The rest of this chapter deals with ways to get out of these habits, from simple nervous habits such as shoulder jerking to more complex desires such as craving for sweets.

NERVOUS HABITS

Nervous habits are simple habits that occur quite automatically, habits such as pulling on eyelashes or facial twitches. They are called nervous habits because for some people they occur more often when the person is nervous. Thus a very important first step in reducing one of your nervous habits is to observe and record (see Chapter 3) whether your habit is triggered by feelings such as nervousness, anxiety, or tension. If this is true, some or most of the time, then you must begin by learning ways to deal with these emotions (see Chapters 6 & 7).

After you have worked with the nervousness or found that the habit is not affected by emotions, then you can reduce or eliminate the habit by the following procedures.

The most important thing is to learn to be more aware of when the habit occurs, particularly since many nervous habits often occur without your knowing it. But with practice you can become more aware of it. And you must be aware in order to stop it. One way to increase this awareness is to count, as with a wrist-counter or written record, every time the habit occurs. This counting makes you more aware. Also you might ask friends or others to point out to you when you are doing the habit.

In addition to counting the habit it is important to do a more complete assessment of it (see Chapter 3). Observe and keep records of the situations in which the habit occurs and any possible things that result from the habit. Pay very careful and detailed attention to the habit so you know all about its different forms in various situations. If there are certain cues that trigger off the habit, consult Chapter 5 (Change of Scene) for possible ways to change these cues.

After assessment the next step is overpractice. This consists of intentionally doing the habit over and over again as realistically as possible. If the habit is shoulder-jerking, then you sit down and intentionally jerk your shoulder over and over in the same way it occurs naturally. Of course, do this in a way that does not hurt you. Thus if your habit is scratching your arm, then you might wear gloves during overpractice.

Overpractice does two things. First it helps you become more aware of whenever the habit occurs. Second it reduces the habit itself to some degree. Sometimes overpractice is enough to eliminate a habit. To get the most out of overpractice you should do it at least once a day for a week or two. And when you do it, you should do it over and over and over again until you feel quite tired of doing it.

The next step is to find an act which is incompatible with the habit, an act which if you do it you can't do the habit. For fingernail biting and eyelash pulling an incompatible act is putting your hands at your sides and clenching your fists or grasping and squeezing an object. For jerking or shaking your head an incompatible act is tensing your neck muscles, perhaps by pulling your chin in and down. An incompatible act for shoulder jerking is pushing your arms and hands down, perhaps against your legs if standing or against your legs or the arms of a chair when sitting. Other examples of incompatible acts are closing the mouth and jaws for cheek and lip biting, relaxing face muscles and blinking intentionally for eye squinting, and dropping jaw and breathing through the mouth for teeth grinding.

Once you determine an incompatible act for your habit, then do this act for 3 minutes every time your habit occurs, for 2 minutes every time you are about to

do your habit, and for one minute every time you are
even tempted to do the habit. Practice using your incompatible act until it becomes a habit and becomes
easy and automatic. This is a critical part of breaking a bad habit.

In addition to using your incompatible act in
real life situations, also spend some time practicing
it in your imagination. From your assessment you know
situations in which your habit often occurs. Sit down,
close your eyes, relax, and imagine yourself in one of
these situations. Notice any tendency for you to do
the habit and if so then practice the incompatible
act. See the next chapter for more on this type of
mental rehearsal.

Finally, if necessary, use some of the motivation
procedures from Chapter 8 to encourage you to do this
change program. If you do all of the above, you can
eliminate any nervous habit you wish.

DESIRES
        A desire is a craving, a yearning, an addiction,
an attachment. It is a felt demand or expectation
that yearns to be satisfied. A desire is based on
something you want. Most people have desires for certain foods, such as eggs, chocolate, or peanut butter.
Most people have desires for one or more drugs such as
caffeine (as in coffee and cola), nicotine, alcohol or
marijuana. Most people have sexual desires related to
certain people, sexual objects, and/or fantasies. Most
people have desires for security, sensation, and power.
Thus everyone has a complex set of desires.

Desires are perfectly natural, but they can easily
get out of control. Examples of desires out of control
include the person driving around at two in the morning
hunting for a place to buy cigarettes, the person who
tends to perceive most people of the opposite sex in
terms of a potential sex object, and the person who
sees other people as he wants them to be rather than
how they are. When some of your desires are out of
control, you become a slave to them. They influence
your perceptions, thoughts, feelings, and actions.
Therefore it is important for everyone to understand
his desires, eliminate some of them (such as a desire
for cigarettes), and get some under control (such as
overeating).

The goal is not to become desireless, but to have

the desires under control. Then you can choose your
activity, rather than it choosing you. Then you can
enjoy life more, being content with what you have
rather than obsessed with what you don't have. The
free and happy person has preferences and likes and
dislikes which affect what he chooses to do, but he is
not thrown about by uncontrolled desires that distort
reality and cause discomfort until they are satisfied.

In fact much of this book deals with desires in
their many forms. Here I summarize a few points and
add some additional ways to work with desires that are
somewhat or largely out of control.

The first step, of course, is to practice observing and recording your desires (see Chapter 3, Know
Yourself). You should see the situations that cue your
desires, external situations as well as your feelings
and thoughts. In some cases you can change some of the
external cues until your desires are under control (see
Chapter 5, Change of Scene). In some cases you can
change your thoughts that cue desires (see Chapter 11,
What Do You Think). Very often desires result from
anxiety, nervousness, or tension. If this is the case,
then these emotions should be dealt with first (see
Chapter 5, Relaxing Body and Mind, and Chapter 6, Calm
and Relaxed Living). In addition to all of this there
are three other approaches for reducing desires: disrupt
the sequence, overloading, and unpleasant associations.

DISRUPT THE SEQUENCE
When a desire begins it often stays until satisfied,
with the person responding like a robot under the control of the desire. Something cues the desire, a sequence of behaviors begins to fulfill the desire, and
this continues until the desire is satisfied. To get
free from this, practice stopping or interrupting this
automatic sequence. When you have a thought about a
snack or something else cues the desire for a snack,
don't immediately and automatically go for the snack.
Either don't get the snack at all or delay getting it
until later. Work on delaying various urges for longer
and longer, until you are choosing what you want, not
jumping to a desire. If there are things you do too
fast, such as eating, slow down and stop occasionally.
Build in pauses of a few minutes. Break free of automatic sequences of behavior.

Learn to play with your desires as you master them.
Sometimes give in to them and sometimes make a point of

not giving in to them. You want to be able to eventually have this choice with little effort or discomfort. Be sure that some of the times when you don't give in to the desire are times when you are giving yourself all sorts of reasons for satisfying the desire. But don't make a big thing of all this; just work with your desires, relax, and observe all your feelings and thoughts.

Approach all of this as a personal challenge, an opportunity to get more free and develop will power. Refuse to be controlled by a desire, such as a desire for a cigarette. Become master of your life.

OVERLOADING
Sometimes when we have too much of something we like, it makes us "sick" of it, so that later we don't want it or perhaps don't even want to think of it. Too many pieces of pie at Thanksgiving can keep us from eating pie for a while. Too many martinis at a friend's party may eliminate our gin drinking for a few days. This is called overloading, consuming something pleasant until it loses its appeal. The effects of overloading may last from a few hours to many years.

You can intentionally overload yourself as a way to break something's hold on you, at least temporarily. If snacking peanuts is your downfall, get a lot of peanuts and eat them until you don't want any more. If you are too caught up in desires for French fries, then eat many French fries for a few days until they lose their hold on you. Overloading usually only has a temporary effect. Thus it is seldom a complete treatment by itself and should be part of a broader program.

You should not use overloading on yourself with dangerous drugs such as alcohol and tobacco. And if you have any concerns about any form of overloading, don't do it or check with your doctor.

UNPLEASANT ASSOCIATIONS
The final way of reducing desires is by associating something unpleasant with them. This is done through the use of imagined, unpleasant scenes. To be effective these scenes often need to be offensive or gross, such as the examples below. In this procedure you sit down, close your eyes, relax, and imagine as realistically as possible a common situation in which the desire arises. For example, a person who wishes to

reduce smoking would imagine a situation in which it is very likely he would have the desire to smoke, such as sitting at the table after dinner or talking on the phone to a friend. You must imagine the scene in detail and experience and live it as if you were actually in the scene, not just seeing yourself in the scene.

While imagining this scene notice the desire arise, notice an intent to do something undesirable. As soon as the desire or intent arises, you now imagine a scene which is very unpleasant to you. For example, the smoker might imagine himself at the dinner table desiring a cigarette, putting a cigarette in his mouth, and then getting sick and vomiting all over himself and the table. The aversive scene must be imagined and experienced in detail.

A person who drinks too much might imagine himself in a favorite bar and then getting drunk and acting in a way he is ashamed of. A person who wishes to reduce homosexual desires might imagine people who are homosexually attractive to him forcing him to drink urine. The aversive scene must be a scene which is aversive to you, such as falling in a cesspool or being attacked by rats. It could also be based on a possible future that might result if you don't control the desire. A smoker might see himself in a nursing home with lung cancer. An overeater might see himself as fat and losing his girlfriend.

This practice should be done almost every day for a few weeks. Each day that you do it, do it a number of times. Imagine several different common situations in which the desire arises. Associate the desire with your unpleasant scene. Live all your imagined scenes in detail. This practice will reduce these desires.

Next, when you are in actual situations that cue the desire, then call up your unpleasant scene. A smoker who feels the desire for a cigarette might imagine getting sick and vomiting. This will reduce the desire for the cigarette. With practice you will find that by doing this you can readily turn off any desires you want. After a moderate amount of experience doing this, you will find you are able to turn off the desire simply by willing it, without needing to use the unpleasant scene. And later on all of this will be automatic (a good habit) and you won't have to pay any attention to it at all.

You have been programmed with various habits and desires. By freeing yourself of this programming you can make your life more free, more happy, and more effective.

SUGGESTED READING

The Azrin and Nunn book gives a comprehensive program for reducing nervous habits such as nail-biting, hair-pulling, and stuttering.

Azrin, N. H. & Nunn, R. G. Habit control in a day. Simon & Schuster, 1977. Pocket Books paperback, 1978.

CHAPTER ELEVEN

WHAT DO YOU THINK?

In this chapter you will learn more about your thinking. You will observe and evaluate your thoughts, identify thinking that works against you, and learn how to control and change your thinking. But first we will consider the importance of positive thinking.

POSITIVE THINKING
If you were to read all of the self-help books and attend all of the personal growth training programs, you would find one principle that is stressed more than any other: the importance and power of positive thinking. If you think of yourself as a person who is physically well or getting better, your health will be better than if you think of yourself as a sick person. If you think of yourself as a friendly, outgoing person, you will be friendlier and more outgoing than if you think of yourself as withdrawn. If you think of living as a happy and exciting adventure, your life will be more pleasant than if you think of living as unpleasant and filled with obstacles. Positive thinking works!! It works for many reasons that go under such words as expectancy, placebo, confidence, and faith.

What you think and believe affects the way you act, which affects how people and the world act to you, which then supports your thinking. If you think of yourself as unhappy, you will act in an unhappy manner. People will then respond to you as an unhappy person, which then convinces you further you are or should be unhappy. On the other hand, if you think of yourself as a happy person, you will act in a happy manner. People will then more enjoy being with you, feel and act happier around you, and respond to you as a happy person. This then strengthens your thoughts of yourself as a happy person, which leads to even more happiness.

How you think affects how you see and react to situations, to people, and to yourself. To a large extent you live in a world of your own thoughts. If these thoughts are negative, you will live in a less pleasant and rewarding world than if the thoughts are positive. Happy people live in a happy world. Unhappy people live in an unhappy world. If your thoughts are filled with fear and hate, you will bring these on yourself. If your thoughts are filled with love and understanding, you will bring these on yourself. This is a universal law found in most major psychologies, religions, and self-help programs. Try it. It will work for you!

Positive thinking is <u>not</u> fooling yourself, trying to convince yourself of something that is not true, or refusing to accept the reality of a situation. Rather it is seeing things as they are from a positive standpoint. Then you may choose to change things, as with the tools you are learning in this book.

BASIC PRINCIPLES
The following are some basic principles for cultivating positive thinking. The more and more you practice these basic principles the happier and more effective your life will become. These are things to <u>do</u>, not just read about. The more you practice these principles the more you will learn about them and about yourself.

1. <u>Live in the here and now</u>. Don't dwell on things in the past which can't be changed. Don't worry about mistakes you made in the past; rather be concerned about making fewer mistakes now. You are only a slave of the past to the extent that you think you are. Let the past go. Be here now. What are you going to do now?

2. <u>Accept yourself</u>. Most negative thinking centers around peoples bad thinking about themselves. Most people are better friends to others than to themselves. Make friends with yourself. See yourself objectively and realistically, including things you want to change. But don't get upset and judgmental by what you see. Accept yourself as you are, for that is reality. A good friend of yours knows many of your strengths and weaknesses, likes and dislikes, and plans for change; and this friend likes you as you are. Make friends with yourself.

3. <u>Develop positive thinking</u>. Practice thinking of yourself and the world in terms of positive, loving images and concepts. Use the tools of the rest of this chapter to better observe your thinking and change it toward more positive thinking.

CHANGING YOUR MIND
Let us consider ways you can learn to think more

positively and generally be able to improve what you think. This involves six basic processes: developing mental flexibility, quieting the mind, observing thinking, evaluating thoughts, reducing undesired thoughts, and increasing desired thoughts.

DEVELOPING MENTAL FLEXIBILITY
In order to improve your thinking, problem-solving ability, and creativity, it is important to cultivate mental flexibility. You need to be ready to change your thinking. It is OK to have been wrong. It is OK to change one's mind. Everyone's mind is somewhat resistant to change. We have a tendency to justify and defend our past and current ideas and beliefs rather than change our minds as better ideas come along. This resistance reduces mental flexibility and slows up personal progress.

Don't hold onto old attitudes, opinions, ideas, and beliefs just because you once considered them important or right. If a better thought comes along, let the past go. Be willing to change your mind. Be willing to have been wrong. This doesn't mean accepting everything that comes along, being gullible, or being unreasonable. Rather it is a matter of being flexible to new thoughts that you consider better, based on your reason and values. Thus you might change your mind about women at your work, issues of national politics, ways to discipline your children, how to be a loving spouse, or what is important for you to accomplish in your life.

QUIETING THE MIND
If the mind is always rushing about like a drunken monkey it is very difficult to observe the thinking and get free from old and troublesome thought patterns. It is important to quiet the mind down and get control of it. Once you have control of it you can use it more effectively as you wish. Ways to quiet and relax the mind are discussed in Chapter 6.

OBSERVING THINKING
Few people observe their thoughts or their thinking processes. Instead they just think. Thus most people spend much of their time lost in thought. But in addition to just thinking, with practice you can learn to also observe the thoughts you think. That is, thoughts are behaviors you can observe just as you observe other of your behaviors such as walking and eating. It would be useful here to review Chapter 3 (Know Yourself) and

73

think about how it applies to your thinking.

Observing your thoughts is a skill to be developed.
The more you practice observing your thoughts, the easier
it will be and the better you will be at it. You will
find out many new and interesting things about yourself
as you observe your thoughts. One point is very important to remember: Observing your thoughts means just
to observe them, not think about them. Thinking about
thoughts is more thinking. Observing your thoughts is
just quietly being aware of your thoughts. Later,
after you have learned to observe your thoughts, you
will be able to observe your processes of thinking.
Here you will find some very basic things about yourself.

As in all cases of learning to observe yourself,
it is useful to use written records, such as a notebook
or log, to record types of thoughts that are of particular interest to you. For example, if anxiety is a
general problem you want to work on, you might keep
records of what you say to yourself when in anxiety
situations and when thinking about anxiety situations.
A useful form for written records about thoughts would
include (1) the situation you are in, (2) the thoughts
you have in this situation, (3) the feelings and actions
that result from these thoughts, and (4) the thoughts
that accompany or follow the feelings and actions.

If you are interested in your smoking, you want to
observe any thoughts that lead to smoking or justify
smoking. If you want to become a more loving person,
you want to observe your thoughts in situations where
you find it difficult to be loving. If you are interested in expanding your consciousness, you should
practice observing your thoughts in all situations.

EVALUATING THOUGHTS
Assuming you have spent some time (ideally a few
weeks) observing and recording your thoughts in situations of importance to you, it is now time to evaluate
the thoughts. Carefully study your written records
of your thoughts. See what you can learn and discover.
What types of thoughts often occur? Which of the
thoughts would you consider undesirable? The first
step in evaluating your thoughts is to determine which
of the thoughts are true or false. Consider a person
who feels anxious at work. After observing and recording anxiety-related thoughts, he finds that the
thought "My boss does not like my work" is a major

source of anxiety. Well, this is the type of thought that should be checked to determine if it is true or false. If false, as many such thoughts are, then it is an unnecessary source of anxiety that should be eliminated. If true, then the question is what should be done to remedy the problem.

If a thought could be true or false, then find out for sure. Get the facts. Ask yourself how you can prove or disprove the thought. What type of evidence would be relevant?

The second type of evaluation is to identify those thoughts that are basically negative, self-defeating, and/or irrational. These are thoughts to be decreased or eliminated, as with the procedures described later. One type of such thoughts are those that are simply untrue. This includes such thoughts as "Healthy people do not get upset" or "Nobody likes me." A second type are those thoughts that are an overgeneralization or overstatement that can't always be true. Examples include "Someone is either with you or against you" and "Every problem has a perfect solution." Other examples include making a generalization about a person based on one thing he does or making a generalization about a group of people based on a few members of the group. A third type are those thoughts which express an unreasonable expectation of yourself. Examples include "I should always be at peak efficiency," "Everyone should like me," and "I should be the perfect parent(or lover, or friend, or...)." A fourth type are those thoughts that are negative in tone, the opposite of positive thinking. Examples are "I wish I were someone else," "If people get to know me, they won't like me," and "Because of my upbringing I can never change."

The following are some very common undesirable thoughts that are negative, self-defeating, and/or irrational. See if any of your thoughts are like any of these. Also think about what is undesirable about each of these thoughts.
Making mistakes shows I am not a good person.
If my opinion is not right, I look like a fool.
It is wonderful to be popular and famous; it is terrible to be mediocre.
If somebody disagress with me, it means he doesn't like me.
It is terrible when things go wrong.
It is necessary to be unhappy now in order to be

happy later.
I have to be unhappy to know when I am happy.
The purpose of life is to work hard, not be happy.
My emotions can not be controlled.
Self-discipline is too hard to achieve.
It is others' responsibility to solve my problems.
Will power alone can solve all of my problems.
Although often self-defeating, anger is unavoidable.
Others may have problems, but they are not like mine.
To ask someone for help is to display weakness.
I can't benefit from professional counseling.
Bad situations only get worse if you stand up to them.
My value as a person depends on what others think
    of me.
I am no good because...
I can't face living because...
I would be really happy if only...
If only...

TAKE ACTION
After observing, recording, and evaluating your
thoughts, it is now time to take some action. Look
at your undesirable thoughts and beliefs and add to
your program for yourself a course of action to offset
them. If many of your thoughts are about not taking
chances, go out of your way to take a chance. If you
tell yourself never to ask for help, practice asking
favors. If you have thoughts and feelings about being
left out of things, then make the first move and don't
wait to be asked. Remember our rule of taking small
steps. Begin by taking small chances or asking small
favors. Then gradually build up to bigger chances or
bigger favors.

Now let's turn to some general ways to decrease
undesired thoughts and increase desired thoughts. This
is important because undesired thoughts are often unpleasant in themselves and because they impair positive
thinking. Also undesired thoughts lead to undesired
feelings and actions, while desired thoughts lead to
desired feelings and actions.

REDUCING UNDESIRED THOUGHTS
The first procedure is thought stopping. This is
a tool to disrupt unwanted thoughts when they come into
your head. It is easy to learn and easy to use. It
may seem a little strange at first; but it will work
well for you. For example, say you did considerable
damage to your new car which really upset you. Now
you find that when you are trying to think of other

things, thoughts of the car keep coming into your mind.
Thought stopping is a way to disrupt this.

The way to do it is to sit quietly, close your
eyes, and let thoughts of the car come into your mind.
As soon as these thoughts appear, shout "STOP" out
loud. You will see this stops the thought. Practice
doing this a few times. Then practice doing it while
you shout "STOP" inside your head, not out loud. If
you practice this for a few days, you will find you
can use it to stop any thoughts you wish. After you
have used thought stopping for a while you will be able
to will thoughts to go away without saying "stop."

You can shout things other than stop. Some people
prefer to shout "GET OUT." Also some people find it
best to shout "STOP" or "GET OUT" three to five times
each time they do it. Other people find it useful at
first to bang their fist on the table when shouting,
while other people wear a rubberband around a wrist
and snap it on the underside of the wrist when they
shout.

Thought stopping is a good way to disrupt and
temporarily stop unwanted thoughts. But for more permanent thought control it is also useful to use negative countering (discussed next) and procedures to increase desired thoughts.

Negative countering is a way of dealing with irrational thoughts. Each time an irrational thought occurs,
you counter it by saying something to yourself which is
contrary to the irrational thought.

One way to do this is by attacking the content of
the thought. If you have problems falling asleep, you
may find that thoughts such as "I'll never get to sleep"
come to mind while trying to get to sleep. Such thoughts
help keep you awake. So when a thought like that occurs
you immediately counter it with another thought such as
"I am resting and will be asleep soon." If the irrational thought is too strong, you use thought stopping
first,followed immediately by negative countering. For
example, in a social situation a person might think
"They are talking about me." If this thought is too
strong for just negative countering, it would be best
to first disrupt the thought with thought stopping and
then use negative countering. If you have an irrational fear in some situations, you may find that when in
those situations, irrational thoughts arise that tell

77

you to be afraid. When such a thought arises, counter it with a thought such as "There is no need for fear in this situation."

A second way of doing negative countering is to attack the irrational thought as being destructive or self-defeating. Now when an irrational thought occurs, you counter it with a thought such as "This thought only hurts me and does not help" or "This thought is pointless" or "This thought gets me in trouble with my friends."

Now make a list of some of your common irrational thoughts. For each one write down a countering statement that makes sense to you. Practice in your imagination doing negative countering. Imagine being in a situation where your irrational thought might occur. Let the thought occur and immediately replace it with your countering statement. Do this imaginary practice on many days for a few weeks. Then start doing negative countering in real life situations whenever irrational thoughts occur. Continue to add irrational thoughts to your list and add or change countering statements.

INCREASING DESIRED THOUGHTS

One way of increasing desired thoughts and positive thinking is through the use of affirmations. These are statements that give you a positive attitude or mood toward such things as the day, your life, or living in general. Below are some popular affirmations. See if any of them speak to you. Find or make up other affirmations which appeal to you.

I have everything in me that I need for what I want to do.
I am wise and knowledgeable and have many talents.
I never have to apologize for being me.
I like myself always and in all ways.
My opinion is as valuable as the next person's.
It is always okay for me to express myself and my feelings in an appropriate way.
I do not judge others but accept them as they are.
I am the lord of my mind and the ruler of my thoughts.
Day by day in every way I am getting better.
I can do all things through Christ who strengthens me.
May I be happy, peaceful, and free from suffering.
I see my problems as opportunities for growth.

After you have one or more affirmations that are suited to you, make a point of saying them to yourself several times each day and several times each time you do it. You might say them to yourself when you get up in the morning, when you go to bed at night, and periodically throughout the day. Some people put their affirmations to a tune so they can sing it out loud or to themselves. It is useful to have signs or reminders to say your affirmations, such as a sign on a cabinet door or a reminder in your wallet or notebook. Over time change your affirmations and add new ones.

A second way of increasing desired thoughts is the use of reasons for change. This consists of making a list of reasons for changing whatever it is you wish to change. Thus if you are working on losing weight, you would make a list of reasons for weight loss, reasons that are true or important to you. Weight loss reasons might include better appearance, increased sexual appeal, better health, longer life, less fatigue, and not being a bad example to the children. If you are trying to avoid spending so much money, your reasons for change might include having a better use for the money, not wanting to borrow money, not being overdrawn at the bank, avoiding money-related fights with your spouse, and the development of self-control of spending.

You should make a list of reasons for change, reasons in your own words that are good reasons for you. Then post this list and each day read through the list and think about the reasons. When you are in a situation and have thoughts going against your change program, such as thoughts to eat or spend too much, then stop these thoughts and mentally review some of your reasons for change. Finally, continually add and subtract from your list of reasons as new reasons come in and old reasons lose some of their strength.

A third way to increase desirable thoughts is by positive countering. This consists of saying positive statements in place of negative ones. The following are examples of positive statements. You could use one or more of these or make up your own.
I am becoming a master of my own life.
I can handle this situation.
I am responsible for my own behavior.
I'm OK.
Many people like me.
I am really a loving person.
I am a considerate person.
It is getting easier to meet people.
I don't need a cigarette.

Now when an undesired thought occurs, you stop it
and replace it with one of these positive countering
statements. Again get out your list of your common
irrational thoughts. Now for each one write down a
positive countering statement that you would use.
Practice using it in your imagination and then practice
using it in real life.

ALL TOGETHER

Putting together the last few sections gives us
this overall approach: Observe and record undesired
thoughts of importance to you. Observe and record the
situations in which these thoughts occur. Next, when
an undesired thought occurs, stop it as soon as possible using thought stopping and/or negative countering. Then immediately replace the undesired thought
with a desired thought such as an affirmation, a reason
for change, or a positive countering statement. You
may wish to carry a list of desired thoughts with you
for use in such situations.

First practice using the above approach in your
imagination. Imagine yourself in various situations
in which the undesired thoughts might occur, let them
happen, and then practice the above approach. After
practicing in your imagination for a number of days,
begin using this approach in real life situations.

Look for ways to reward yourself for all of this:
reward yourself for practicing thought stopping and
positive and negative countering, reward yourself for
saying your affirmations, and be sure to reward yourself
whenever you apply this in a real life situation. The
reward might be praising yourself or feeling personally
satisfied, the reward might be a little treat of some
type, or the reward might be a mark in your notebook
to be added to other marks for a bigger reward. Chapter
8 (Getting Motivated) discusses various ways to reward
yourself.

TALKING TO YOURSELF

Although talking to yourself out loud is not always a good idea, everybody talks to themselves in
their heads. Talking to yourself, when done in a
positive and helpful manner, can be a very useful
thing to do. One good example is learning to ask yourself questions about various situations. What will be
expected of me at the meeting? What sort of things
should I expect at the party? Have I had too many
drinks? Such questions help you think things through

and plan ahead.

Another good form of talking to yourself consists of giving yourself instructions about various situations. Examples include the following: Relax. Listen. Stop and think. Stop thinking nonsense. Think positively. Be less critical. I don't need to prove myself. Getting upset won't help. I'm not going to let him get to me. Slow down eating and pay more attention. Drink slowly and take smaller sips.

What you think influences how you feel and act. Use this chapter to learn more about your own thinking and how you can make it more positive and useful. This will help make your life more pleasant and more productive.

SUGGESTED READING

The first two books (Ellis & Harper, Lazarus & Fay) discuss irrational assumptions and undesirable self-statements and suggest some ways for dealing with them. Maltz's book emphasizes the influence of a person's self-image on his personality and behavior. Maltz suggests ways to use the imagination to reprogram the self-image. Newman's book similarly deals with a person's attitudes, self-concept, and self-esteem. He also utilizes the imagination and suggests ways to re-program the unconscious. Burns' book deals with overcoming depression.

Ellis, A. & Harper, R. A. A new guide to rational thinking. Wilshire Book Co., 1975.
Lazarus, A. & Fay, A. I can if I want to. William Morrow & Co. 1975. Warner Books paperback, 1977.
Maltz, M. Psychocybernetics. Prentice-Hall, 1960. Pocket Book paperback, 1969.
Newman, J. W. Release your brakes! Warner Books paperback, 1978.
Burns, D. D. Feeling good. Signet paperback, 1981.

CHAPTER TWELVE

MENTAL REHEARSAL

Mental rehearsal is the practice of imagining what you are going to do or say in a future situation. It is a common, powerful practice that helps you be prepared and overcome obstacles. If you are going to ask your boss for a raise, it may be useful to practice beforehand in your imagination what you are going to say and how you will respond to different things he might say. If there is a person who gets you angry by his kidding, you can practice in advance how you might handle this kidding without getting angry, particularly if getting you angry is a main reason he kids you.

Mental rehearsal is a very old technique that has been practiced for centuries in many cultures. You will find it very useful and easy to do if you follow these four steps: relax, live realistic scenes, practice variations, and take small steps into the world.

1. <u>Relax</u>. Mental rehearsal should be done when your are relaxed and have plenty of time for the practice. Close your eyes and relax your body and mind, as with the procedures of Chapter 6. While relaxed do mental rehearsal as described below. If at any time you notice yourself becoming non-relaxed, such as anxious or tense, stop the mental rehearsal and relax. After relaxing you may start mental rehearsal again.

2. <u>Live realistic scenes</u>. In mental rehearsal you want to imagine situations as realistically as possible. Make the imagined scene as detailed as possible and use as many different senses in your imagination as possible. If you are imagining asking your boss for a raise, then imagine <u>in detail</u> what it is like to enter the boss' office. See the details of the office and your boss. See the details change as you come in and sit down. Use other senses in your imagination if possible. Hear yourself knock on the door. Hear the boss talk to you. Feel the chair as you sit down. During all of this it is very important that you <u>live</u> these scenes! Do not just imagine yourself in the situation as if you were watching yourself on a movie screen. Rather, be in the scene and live it as realistically as you can.

3. <u>Practice variations</u>. Practice different varia-

tions of the situations you are mentally rehearsing.
Practice with variations of the place. Practice with
variations of how the people react to you and what they
say. For each situation practice what you would say
to yourself (see Chapter 11), what you would say to
others, and what you would do. This practice with variations prepares you for the various things you might
encounter. Consider a person who is easily talked into
spending too much. Mental rehearsal for him might consist of visualizing sales situations and salespeople
and how to handle them. Variations would include imagining being in different stores and imagining different
things salespeople might say. Mental rehearsal would
include imagining what would be said to these various
salespeople, being polite but resisting buying. Or
consider an unassertive person who feels uncomfortable
asking a waitress for extra service,such as more sour
cream for his potato. Mental rehearsal would consist
of realistically imagining being in a particular res-
taurant and wanting more sour cream. Practicing variations would include imagining different conditions
of the restaurant (slow to busy) and different reactions of the waitress (friendly to unfriendly). Mental
rehearsal here would reduce the anxiety and give the
person practice in what to do or say in various situations.

    4. Take small steps into the world. Remember our
general strategy of taking small steps. After you have
practiced mental rehearsal it is often useful to gradually approach the real world situation. For example,
if your mental rehearsal has centered around resisting
pressure to spending money, the first step into the
real world might be to go to low pressure stores with
just a little money. Then you can gradually work up
to more difficult situations. If you have trouble
asking a waitress for extra service, then start with
a small request to a friendly waitress at a non-busy
time. Then work up to harder situations.

    During mental rehearsal and going into the world
stay in tune with your feelings and thoughts. If you
start to feel an unwanted emotion, such as anxiety or
anger, notice it, relax, and practice turning it off
as best you can. If your thoughts become irrational,
negative, or self-defeating, notice them, relax, and
practice replacing them with positive thoughts.

EXAMPLES
    Bob was concerned about the working conditions at

84

his office and had ideas for improvement. But he felt
very anxious about suggesting his ideas to his supervisor, a bright woman who was usually very busy and
seemed easily bothered when someone interrupted her
work. Bob felt anxious around her and usually did not
say exactly what he wanted. With mental rehearsal Bob
practiced approaching her and making some suggestions.
This allowed him to reduce much of the anxiety and practice what to say in various situations. Then Bob worked
out a gradual set of steps for the real world, starting
with just saying hello to his supervisor, to a short
chat, to making a minor suggestion, and eventually to
discussing with her some of his real concerns. When
he was done he had eliminated the anxiety, developed
a better relationship with his supervisor, and improved
his working conditions.

Ann often got upset by Jack's sexist attitude
toward her. However, getting upset caused her not to
deal with Jack in the best way. She would later think
of a better thing to have said or done. Using mental
rehearsal she practiced various ways to respond to Jack
without getting upset. This helped her deal with Jack
more effectively and reduce his sexist approach.

Mental rehearsal can also help skills such as hit-
ting a tennis ball or playing music. This is a common
practice among professional athletes and musicians. For
example, a golfer might mentally rehearse playing a few
holes of golf, realistically imagining a particular
course, the weather conditions, the lie of the ball on
a particular hole, the club in his hand, and the hit-
ting of the ball. Such mental rehearsal, if realistically imagining the correct way to play, may improve
his golf game.

VARIATIONS
Finally, there are some variations of mental rehearsal that might be useful to you.

Small steps in the imagination. When imagining a
situation in mental rehearsal you might find that you
feel a moderate or large amount of anxiety, or some
other unwanted emotion. Or you might find that when
such an emotion occurs, it is difficult to relax and
shut it off. In either case you should apply our strategy of small steps to the imagined scene. That is,
start your mental rehearsal with a scene that only
causes a little anxiety (or whatever emotion), and
practice turning it off and relaxing. Then gradually

85

imagine scenes that cause more and more anxiety. But don't move to a new scene until you can imagine the current scene without feeling anxious. If you use small steps during mental rehearsal, it is very important that you use a lot of small steps when going into the world.

Imagining others. If at first you find it difficult or unrealistic to imagine yourself doing something, then start by imagining someone else doing it. Pick someone who has the characteristic you wish to develop and/or acts the way you wish to act. This person could be a friend, celebrity, athlete, religious figure, or someone else you respect or admire. If you have a choice of different people, pick the one who is most similar to you. Now your mental rehearsal should have three stages and you should master each stage before going to the next: (1) imagine this other person acting appropriately in the various situations of concern to you; (2) imagine seeing yourself, as on a screen, doing what the other person did; and then (3) live and experience the scene, imagining yourself actually acting, talking, feeling and thinking the way you wish.

Imagining others can be readily combined with taking small steps in the imagination. Here you begin by imagining the other person gradually dealing with more and more difficult situations. Then you imagine yourself in the same gradual sequence of situations.

Role-reversal. Role-reversal consists of imagining being someone else in one of the situations you are using for mental rehearsal. That is, you imagine yourself in the role of one of the people you have trouble with. Thus you might imagine yourself as your boss being asked for a raise. Or you might imagine yourself as a very busy waitress being asked for more sour cream. Role-reversal is something you would do periodically along with your mental rehearsal. Role-reversal helps you better see from the other person's point of view and recognize some of his problems. This then helps you better understand others and interact with them more effectively.

SUGGESTED READING

Lazarus' book describes the use of imagery and mental rehearsal for a variety of personal problems, including overcoming anxiety and being more assertive.

Lazarus, A. In the mind's eye: The power of imagery
for personal enrichment. Rawson, 1978.

CHAPTER THIRTEEN

NUTRITION AND EXERCISE

Although the emphasis of this book is psychological, it is important to remember that the body and mind strongly influence each other. Thus the condition of your body affects how you feel and how you think. For example, if you are sick you might be more irritable and not think as well. Or if your body is sluggish and out of condition, then your style of living may be sluggish and your thinking may be sluggish. On the other hand, getting your body physically fit will probably improve the way you feel about yourself, give you more energy, and lead to being more alert.

GETTING IN TOUCH

Most people are surprisingly out of touch with their bodies. They are not aware how many of the things they do affect their bodies. And they are not aware of the ways their bodies affect their minds. Thus the first step is to get more in touch with your body. Make friends with your body. Treat your body as a temple to be respected and kept clean and in good shape.

Pay more attention to your body. Practice being more aware of your feelings: how they start, how they feel,how they change over time, and how they influence your thinking. Practice being aware of how psychological conditions, such as anxiety and tension, affect different parts of your body. Practice being aware of how different physical activities affect your psychological condition. Here the procedures of Chapters 6 and 7 (Relaxing Body and Mind, Calm and Relaxed Living) should be useful.

Learn how the following affect your moods and the way your body feels: what you eat and drink, things you smoke, any drugs you use, different types of exercise, and aspects of the climate, such as temperature and humidity. Experiment with yourself by changing some of these things and noticing the differences. Alter your diet for a while and see how it influences your mood. Eliminate an unnecessary drug (such as alcohol) for a month or so and notice changes in your body and mind.

Get in touch with your body. Treat it well. Make friends with yourself.

NUTRITION

What you eat and drink has a tremendous effect on your body and mind. For example, not getting enough of some vitamins can cause such things as poor vision, circulatory problems, skin problems, lack of appetite, diarrhea, headaches, sleeplessness, impaired memory, nervousness, irritability, and mental confusion. In some cases a person is not getting enough of the vitamins in the foods he eats and thus needs to change his diet and/or take vitamin supplements. In some cases a person's body has a deficiency in being able to utilize the vitamins in his diet. This person might need more vitamin supplements than the average person.

Lack of adequate protein in your diet can lead to lack of energy and slower reactions. Inadequate protein in a child's diet might lead to brain damage and/or failure of the brain to reach its potential.

Change in a person's blood sugar level can have dramatic effects on moods, such as causing a person to feel very depressed. Thus many people, particularly people with diabetes and hypoglycemia, need to learn how their diet affects their blood sugar level and how this affects their moods. For example, if a person with hypoglycemia eats too many carbohydrates it causes a decrease in blood sugar level below what is needed. This then could lead to symptoms such as being weak, nervous, irritable, or aggressive. It can lead to the person being overweight yet undernourished. (Similar symptoms could have many other causes such as some diseases and infections or problems in a neurological or endocrine system.) If hypoglycemia is identified by a doctor, it may be treated with a high protein, low carbohydrate diet.

For some people, moderate to large amounts of caffeine can lead to nervousness, irritability, and insomnia. Caffeine is often found in coffee, tea, cola drinks, cocoa, and aspirin. For some children food additives, such as artificial coloring, may lead to hyperactivity, a general nervousness and difficulty in staying still.

There are great individual differences in how people react to food. A person can have a strong reaction or allergy to something usual or unexpected. For example, for one person eating chocolate may cause him to be more aggressive. There are also many foods that might cause headaches: fats, fried foods, chocolate, wine, oranges, MSG (monosodium glutamate), nitrates (as in hot dogs and other processed meats), to mention only a few possibilities.

Thus it is very important for you to learn how what you eat and drink affects you. The above examples are just a few examples of many. You need to experiment with yourself and learn how nutrition affects you.

GENERAL NUTRITION PRINCIPLES

Learning more about nutrition can be very helpful to you. Unfortunately there are many different, often contradictory, points of view about what is good nutrition. These points of view are influenced by cultural differences, research findings, personal experiences, and religious beliefs. The books in the suggested reading at the end of this chapter provide a sample of some of the different points of view. I leave it to you to decide. However, there are some general principles of good nutrition.

First, as mentioned above, is the importance of experimenting with your diet to find how what you eat affects you. However, if you have any question about any of this, or if you are considering any dramatic change, be sure to check with your doctor or nutrition specialist.

Become more aware of exactly what you are eating. Carefully read labels of ingredients. Note that the ingredients listed first are generally those in the highest amounts. Watch for artificial preservatives and additives. Notice how often sugar is an ingredient! Be careful of too much sugar and/or salt. Be careful of highly processed foods, where many nutrients are lost in the processing and then some are added back in. If someone other than you fixes the meals, ask about what went into the meals. Be careful of overcooking foods as this often can result in loss of many nutrients.

Eat a balanced diet. Be sure you get enough of the basic nutrients: carbohydrates, fats, protein, vitamins, minerals and water. Also eat enough raw foods and fiber. Some unbalanced diets, such as some weight-loss diets and some "spiritual" diets, could be harmful to your body.

Finally, moderation is generally good advice. Be wary of anything you eat or drink a lot of, such as soft drinks or candy. Consider reducing all excesses

91

and in some cases try removing the problem food from your diet for a few weeks.

WEIGHT LOSS

There are three basic variables that influence your weight: eating habits, calorie intake, and exercise. If you take in more calories than you use up, you gain weight. If you use up more calories than you take in, you lose weight.

Thus exercise, discussed below, is an important component of a weight loss program, since exercise uses up calories. However, exercise by itself is not enough, since most people do not or can not exercise enough to offset the calories they can easily take in. A piece of cake can quickly offset the calories used up in an hour of exercising. Therefore it is necessary to become more aware of the calories you take in and find ways to reduce these calories. The best way to do this is by changing your eating habits as discussed in Chapter 16 (Eating and Weight Control).

If you wish to lose weight, change your eating habits, exercise, and reduce the calories you consume. Learn how to determine the calories in what you eat: see the calories listed on labels, get a book that gives calories for various foods, and learn to estimate the amount of food. Reduce the calories you consume, but don't eat an unbalanced diet. Reduce the calories you take in, but not below the needs of your body, which for many people is at least 1200 calories per day. Check with your doctor or nutrition specialist about the calories your body size needs and the effects of any weight loss or special diet. Finally, remember that reducing calories need not mean less appealing food. Find other good tasting food and recipes with fewer calories.

EXERCISE

As mentioned above, exercise can help you feel better, both physically and mentally. Exercise can be good recreation and relaxation which helps your mental and emotional well-being. Other possible benefits of exercise include better balance and coordination, less fatigue, sounder sleep, reduced emotional tensions, better sex life, lower blood pressure, and longer life. But you must be patient! Many of these benefits you may not begin to notice until after a couple of months of exercise.

Next let us consider five different goals of exercise: general conditioning, muscle tone and posture, flexibility, burning calories, and meditation.

GENERAL CONDITIONING
        General conditioning, also called aerobic conditioning, is exercise that strengthens the respiratory and cardiovascular systems. Strengthening the respiratory system increases lung capacity and improves breathing. Exercising the cardiovascular system strengthens the heart (which is a muscle) and improves circulation, as by enlarging and strengthening the arteries and by slowing the build-up of cholesterol. General conditioning thus improves the overall health and functioning of your body. It is the form of exercise that is probably the most useful for most people.

        The general conditioning (aerobic) exercises are those that increase your heart rate and cause deeper or heavier breathing. Your doctor or physical fitness expert can help you pick the exercises that are right for you relative to your present physical condition. You can learn how to take your pulse to monitor the effects of exercise.

        Good general conditioning exercises include walking, running, jogging, bicycling, swimming, skating,cross country skiing, jumping rope, dancing, and many running sports such as tennis and racquetball. There are many good aerobic books on these and other exercises. Usually these exercises are best done in a rhythmic, repetitive, and sustained manner. That is, continually and smoothly do the exercise for a period of time each time you do it. It is usually good to do general conditioning exercises three or four times a week.

MUSCLE TONE AND POSTURE
        It is useful to do a variety of exercises that use a variety of different muscles and develop muscle tone. These exercises help keep the muscles in good shape and health and ready for use when needed. It is important to do a wide variety of exercises so that you work with as many different muscles as possible. Calisthenics and isometrics are good exercises for muscle tone, as are more general exercises such as walking and swimming.

        In addition you may want to do specialized work on certain muscles. You may want to develop muscles that have gotten weak due to disuse, an accident, or an operation. You may want to strengthen muscles to prevent possible problems such as strengthening muscles to keep a joint from dislocating. Or you may want to work with muscles to improve your appearance such as situps to tighten your stomach. When losing weight it is useful to shape up your figure or physique.

Good posture is important to help hold organs in their proper place and help them function more effectively. Become more aware of how you hold your body, as when walking and sitting. Look for ways to improve your posture, such as keeping your back more vertical and not leaning or slouching in any direction.

FLEXIBILITY
Flexibility is the ability of the body to easily move in many different ways in a wide range of directions. Many young children have great flexibility because they do a wide variety of activities. As people get older they become more restricted in how they move their bodies; and so they gradually lose flexibility. When a person leaves his teens he needs to pay more attention to flexibility. A common error for people in their 30's and older is to emphasize muscle tone too much and flexibility not enough. Flexibility also helps minimize sports injuries.

The key to flexibility is to do a wide variety of body movements that emphasize moving in natural, non-harmful ways in which you usually don't move. The best flexibility exercises are slow, rhythmic stretching exercises in which you stop at the point of any discomfort. Exercises specifically geared toward flexibility include aspects of calisthenics, dancing, yoga body positions (specifically hatha yoga), and martial arts such as karate and tai chi.

BURNING CALORIES
All exercise uses up calories which helps in weight loss and weight control. The exercises which burn up the most calories are those that require the most total work, not necessarily the most speed or vigor. The general conditioning exercises listed above are good calorie burners.

Some people who are trying to lose weight are concerned that exercise will cause them to "work up an appetite" and eat more. In fact it usually works the other way around. Exercising before a meal may decrease your appetite. Exercising in general may overall cause

you to be less hungry. Active people often eat less
than inactive people.

MEDITATION
Your physical exercise can also be a meditation
exercise (see discussion of meditation in Chapter 6).
When exercising, gently keep your attention on the
exercise: how your body feels, how you are breathing,
how your body moves. If other thoughts or sensations
come to mind, such as plans for later in the week or
worrying about some problem, notice these thoughts or
sensations and then gently bring your attention back
to your exercising.

Depending on the type of exercising you are doing,
look for opportunities to do things such as the following: Be more aware of the feelings of breathing,
your diaphragm rising and falling, your chest going in
and out, and the flow of air through nose, mouth,
throat, and lungs. Be more aware of the many feelings
in your body, including sensing, touching, holding,
stretching, pushing, working, tiring, and relaxing. Be
more aware of the movement of your body. Notice in
detail all of the various sensations involved in even
the simplest movement. Be more aware of how your body
moves around in the space you are in.

Let your movements become more fluid and graceful.
Many exercises can be treated as a fluid art form, exercises such as running, swimming, dancing, and bowling.
If the exercise involves equipment such as a racket or
bat, let the equipment become an extension of your body.
Rather than the racket just being something you are
holding, let it feel as if it is part of your body.

Gently keep your attention on the feelings of the
exercise. Pay attention to how your body actually
feels, not how you think it feels. Practice being
totally in the here and now of the exercise, not
remembering things from the past or planning for the
future. Immerse yourself in the exercise so the exercise is something your body is doing smoothly and
naturally, rather than something you are telling your
body to do. But don't be so lost in your exercise you
lose awareness of other things around you. This is a
time to be more aware of everything, with emphasis on
your body.

GENERAL EXERCISE PRINCIPLES
As a general rule it is important for you to check

with your physical fitness expert and/or doctor about what exercises are appropriate for you, given your condition, age, physiological limitations, and needs. This is particularly true if you have any heart or lung problems, high blood pressure, or diabetes, if you are overweight, or if you smoke more than a pack of cigarettes a day. For example, some aerobic and isometric exercises would not be good for some people with heart problems. Some flexibility exercises are not good for some people with spinal cord limitations.

Take small steps. Gradually build up. If you have done little exercise for a while, don't try to go out and run a mile. Perhaps walk before you jog. Perhaps run or jog a while before joining a basketball team. Take small steps. Train, don't strain. Do warm up exercises before doing heavy exercise. And then don't sit down right after exercise. Walk around and cool down.

Practice being more aware of your body. When the exercise permits, for part of the time practice focusing your attention on your breathing. Pay more attention to your breathing. Pay more attention to various feelings in your body. Practice getting more in touch with your body. Befriend yourself.

Have some variety in your exercise program. This will help you have a well-rounded program that works with different parts of your body. Altering your exercise program may also keep it more interesting and fun. However, if you have a form of exercise you really enjoy and profit from, then stay with it and vary your other exercises. You may wish to have substitute exercises. For example, you might have a program of three aerobic exercises a week. Most of the time you jog, but occasionally you substitute a certain amount of swimming for jogging. When working on your arm muscles you might be able to substitute push-ups and pull-ups for the usual isometrics.

Look for ways to increase the overall amount of exercise in your daily life. Be wary of too many "labor-saving" devices. The following are some possible ways to do this: Walk instead of ride. When you drive, park further away and walk more. Take stairs instead of elevators. During the day take exercise breaks rather than coffee breaks. Look for more family fun activities that involve exercise. Stand on one foot while putting on your shoes and socks.

Do isometrics while riding the bus. Do the house-
cleaning at a faster rate and/or work harder.

Finally, if you have trouble getting yourself
to do exercises, then apply the motivating techniques
of Chapter 8 (Getting Motivated), which will help you
get going.

SUGGESTED READING

NUTRITION
     The books below give you a sample of some of the
major approaches to nutrition. Airola stresses less
animal protein and more seeds, nuts, grains, vegetables,
and fruits. He also recommends periodic juice fasting.
Ballentine provides an excellent survey of nutrition
and also combines Western science and Eastern yoga. In
addition to sections on the ecology, biochemistry, phys-
iology and pharmacology of nutrition, there is also
a section on food and consciousness. Ballentine suggests a balanced diet could include drawing from the
following five food groups, in approximate decreasing
order of amount: grains, vegetables, legumes, raw food,
food with vitamin B12. The Kirschmann book covers
basic nutrition, nutrients helpful for various ailments,
and the nutrients in various foods. Lappe discusses
the need and way to get protein without meat.

Airola, P. Are you confused. Health Plus Publishers,
     1971
Ballentine, R. Diet and nutrition: a holistic
     approach. Himalayan International Institue, 1978.
Kirschmann, J. D. (ed.). Nutrition almanac. McGraw-
     Hill, revised edition, 1979.
Lappe, F. M. Diet for a small planet. Ballentine
     paperback, revised edition 1975. See also the
     companion volume: Ewald, E. G. Recipes for a
     small planet. Ballentine paperback, 1973.

EXERCISE
     The Cooper book is one of several aerobic books
by Cooper and his associates. These are the best
aerobic books. Hittleman's book is one of several
good introductions to yoga body exercises. The Solomon
and Harrison book is one of several good general exercise books.

Cooper, K. H. The aerobic way. Evans, 1977. Bantam
     Paperback, 1978.

Hittleman, R. Introduction to yoga. Workman, 1969.
    Bantam Paperback, 1979.
Solomon, N. & Harrison, E. Doctor Solomon's proven
    master plan for total body fitness and maintenance.
    Putnam's Sons, 1976. Berkley Medallion Paperback,
    1978.

CHAPTER FOURTEEN

INTRODUCTION TO SECTION THREE

This section shows you how you can use the skills you have learned so far to handle some common problems. Each chapter deals with a special problem, shows you how to apply what you have learned, and provides new information about working with the problem. Therefore you should be quite familiar with the material from the last section before beginning this section. It would also be useful at this time to reread Chapter 2 about basic strategy and think about how what is said applies to you and your goals.

It would be worthwhile to read all the chapters of this section, even if they do not seem to apply to you. For as you see how the strategies and tools of this book are applied to different problems, you will better see how they apply to things of importance to you. For example, the next chapter deals with fears. But even if you do not have any fears you wish to reduce, the approach for dealing with fears can be applied to any unwanted emotion, such as anger or jealousy.

GENERAL REFERENCES

These are books that cover some of the topics of the last section and some of the problem areas of this section. More specialized references are given at the end of the chapters of this book.

Rathus, S. A. & Nevid, J. S. BT-Behavior therapy. Doubleday, 1977. Signet paperback, 1978.
Robbins, J. & Fisher, D. How to make and break habits. Wyden, 1973. Dell paperback, 1976.
Schmidt, J. A. Help yourself. Research Press, 1976.
Tasto, D. L. & Skjei, E. W. Spare the couch. Prentice-Hall, 1979.

CHAPTER FIFTEEN

FEARS

Just about everyone experiences some fears, situations or thoughts that cause anxiety and insecurity. Common examples are fears of spiders, snakes, flying, heights and the dark. Other common sources of anxiety include interacting with some people, speaking before groups, taking tests, and worrying about death. This chapter shows you how to reduce unwanted fears.

Some fears are helpful and should be left alone. If you are anxious about riding in a car with a drunk driver, this is a realistic fear. This fear can be helpful if it keeps you out of a dangerous situation and/or gets you to encourage drunk people not to drive. Fears like this should usually be left alone. However, if the fear is too strong, you may wish to reduce it somewhat with the procedures below.

Some fears are based on misinformation or misperception. Here the fear is due to false information. So, before you start worrying, get the facts. If you are afraid of cats because you believe they will jump at you and scratch you, get the facts. Do cats really jump and scratch? Are you in any real danger from the cats you encounter? If you are afraid to make suggestions to your supervisor because you believe it will make her angry, get the facts. How do you know suggestions will anger her? Isn't there a way suggestions could be made without causing anger? Get the facts!

If you think there is a possibility you might be misperceiving a situation, ask other people what they perceive. Ask your co-workers whether they think the supervisor is angered by suggestions. What kind of suggestions? In what situations? Quieting your mind is a good way to reduce misperception (see Chapter 6). Getting the facts and clearing up misperceptions will reduce many fears. In some cases this is all you will need to do. In other cases there will still be additional anxiety to be reduced by the procedures in this chapter.

Some fears are primarily caused by what you think. Negative and irrational thoughts may come to mind and make you anxious. This type of anxiety is best reduced by the procedures of Chapter 11 (What Do You Think?).

101

Finally, some fears are so strong or so complex that you can not treat them by yourself. Or the fear may be too personal for you to objectively deal with it by yourself. In these cases you may wish to seek professional help, preferably someone whose approach is similar to that described in this chapter and Chapter 11 (What Do You Think?)

However, you can effectively reduce or eliminate most fears by yourself, using the procedures of this book. These procedures have been well-researched and shown to be very effective. With a little time and patience you can reduce your fears and have a much more pleasant life.

The rest of this chapter deals with the basic procedure for reducing fears, or any other unwanted emotion. I'll use the word "anxiety" in this chapter as an example of any unwanted emotion. The procedure has three steps: (1) Learn to relax. (2) While relaxed, gradually approach the feared situation in your imagination. (3) While relaxed, gradually approach the feared situation in real life.

RELAX
    The first step is to spend a few weeks learning to relax as described in Chapter 6 (Relaxing Body and Mind). While doing these relaxation practices, proceed to get to know your fear.

KNOW YOUR FEAR
    To reduce your fear you need to know it pretty well: when it arises, how you feel, what you think, and how you act. The better you know your fear, the better you can reduce or eliminate it. Here is how to do it.

    First let us consider the case where you get anxious several times a week or day and have some idea about what causes the anxiety. The first thing to do is to work at being more and more aware of all the times this particular fear or anxiety occurs. Try to be an objective witness of yourself being anxious. Observe all the different ways the anxiety affects you. Be glad to have the opportunity to learn about your fears and anxieties. Do not make yourself worse by getting angry with yourself or more anxious because you feel a fear or anxiety! This is a common trap. A person will become anxious, notice he is anxious, become anxious about being anxious, and thus cause himself to be even more anxious. Avoid this trap.

The next step is to keep a written log. Chapter 3
(Know Yourself) describes different types of logs and
the advantages of them. Your anxiety log should have
the following headings: Situations, Feelings, Thoughts,
Behavior, and Reactions of Others. As soon as possible
after each time you feel the fear or anxiety, get out
your log and fill it in as described next.

Situations. In this column put a description of
the situation where the anxiety arose. Include the
place, people, and what was going on. This information
will be useful many ways. First, it will provide examples for the anxiety hierarchy you will be developing
later. Second, it may suggest ways of altering your
world to reduce anxiety (see Chapter 5, Change of Scene).
You may find there are ways you can change some situations so they won't cause as much anxiety.

Feelings. In this column describe exactly how you
felt in the situation. Did you feel anxious, fearful,
frustrated, or something else? Then give a number
between 0 and 100 to how strong your feelings were.
Zero corresponds to very relaxed, calm and peaceful,
while 100 corresponds to the most anxious (or whatever
feeling) you can imagine.

The information in this column will help you get
more in touch with your feelings. But regardless of
how you label your undesired feelings (anxiety, anger,
or whatever), the procedures of this chapter will help
you reduce or eliminate them. Assigning numbers to the
feelings is useful in two ways. First, it will be used
later in making your anxiety hierarchy. Second, it will
help identify those situations that cause the most anxiety. If possible, you may wish to avoid some of these
high anxiety situations until you have developed the
skills to deal with them, as described below.

Thoughts. In this column write down any thoughts
you had when in the anxiety situation. What were you
thinking? What did you say to yourself? After you
have kept your log for a week or two, look carefully
at this column. Did your thoughts make the anxiety
worse? Were your thoughts primarily responsible for
you getting anxious? Was the situation really not
anxiety-producing but you made it so by what you told
yourself? If there is any chance your thoughts affect
your anxiety, then review the procedures of Chapter 11

(What Do You Think?) and reduce anxiety-producing thoughts and increase anti-anxiety thoughts.

Behavior. In this column write down how you acted in this situation after you became anxious. After keeping track of this information for a while, you want to ask yourself questions such as the following: What is the effect of anxiety on how I act? Do I need to learn better ways of handling anxiety? Does the way I act cause me to feel anxious? Am I anxious about how I will act when I am anxious?

Reactions of Others. In this column write down how other people reacted to your behavior listed in the previous column. After a week or two of these records see what you can learn about the influence of other people. For example, if when you are anxious do some of your friends or family give your extra attention, concern, or love? If so, this may be one of the reasons you get anxious. You are rewarded with love and attention for getting anxious. In this case you want to encourage your friends not to support your anxiety, but rather support your program to reduce anxiety.

Keep a detailed log, as described above, for at least one week and preferably longer before going further with the anxiety-reducing procedures of this chapter. After you have kept the log for a while and looked back over it, you will probably discover a number of interesting things about your anxiety and yourself. It would be very useful to continue keeping your log even after you have begun the anxiety-reducing procedures. For this will continually provide more useful information for your program, help you identify areas where your program needs to be altered, and provide you a way of observing your progress.

INFREQUENT SPECIFIC FEARS
Some fears are very specific, such as fear of flying, taking tests, or public speaking, yet don't come up very often. In these cases just keeping a log for a week or two may not give you much information about the fears. There are two ways to develop a log for such fears. One is to put yourself in the fearful situation, if it is not too fearful or dangerous, and observe your feelings, thoughts, and behaviors and the reactions of others. Thus you might volunteer to give a short speech or you might go to the airport and pretend you are going to take a flight.

104

The second approach is to relax, close your eyes, and realistically imagine being in the fearful situation (taking a test, flying in a plane). Do this for the whole situation, from beginning to end, such as parts of a whole plane flight from boarding to getting off. Do this many times with different variations of the situations, such as taking tests in different courses or flying in different types of weather.

Through one or both of these approaches, putting yourself in the situation and/or imagining it, you can get to know your fear better and develop a log.

NON-SPECIFIC FEARS

Sometimes a person may feel anxious quite a bit but not be able to identify a particular fear or source of anxiety. If this seems true for you, there are three possible solutions.

It may be that there are one or more types of situations that cause anxiety, but you are not aware of what these are. To check this out keep a log as described above, for all situations in which you feel anxious. Keep the log for two to three weeks and then look for what is common to the various anxiety situations. Group the situations into two or more categories that describe the common causes of anxiety. For example, one category of situations might be fear of public criticism, another might be fear of losing control, and a third might be anxiety about looking foolish. Each category can then be treated as a separate fear and dealt with using the procedures below.

If you have trouble finding categories that fit your anxiety situations and/or you are coming up with a large number of fears or categories, then you should put your emphasis on the procedures described in Chapter 7 (Calm and Relaxed Living).

Finally, if you can't find any causes for your anxiety, it seems independent of situations and thoughts, then you might consider the possibility that the cause is physiological. Be honest with yourself. Don't assume it is physiological because you are avoiding the real causes. But some anxiety can be due to physiological sources. The first thing to consider here is your nutrition, as described in Chapter 13 (Nutrition and Exercise). After that consult your doctor or a neurologist. But be very careful here, for many causes of anxiety that are diagnosed as physiological

are really not. And even if the cause is physiological,
the best treatment usually includes many of the approaches of this book.

Now for those of you who have kept a log and
identified some of the sources of anxiety, it is time
to develop an anxiety hierarchy.

ANXIETY HIERARCHY
The idea of an anxiety hierarchy is to take the
situations that cause anxiety and put them in a list
ranked in order of how much anxiety they cause. Then
you can gradually work through the list starting with
the situations that cause the least anxiety. As your
anxiety reduces and your ability to reduce anxiety
gets stronger, you will gradually be able to deal with
situations you could not have handled before.

Take the anxiety situations from your log and put
them all in one list or one list for each category of
sources of anxiety. The first in the list should be
the situation which causes the least anxiety. The
second is the situation which cuases the second least
amount of anxiety. And so on to the last item which
causes the most anxiety. The 0 to 100 ratings of your
feelings in the various situations should help in this
ordering.

Now carefully look over your list. Are the items
really in the right order. If not, make the necessary
changes. Next see how many situations are on your
list. A good number is 15 to 20. If you have more
than this, fine. If you have much less than this, it
would be good to add some more situations. You might
be able just to think of some more situations. Or you
might make some variations of items on your list to
give you some more items. Or you might come up with
more items as you keep your log longer.

The next step is to look carefully at your hierarchy and see if there are any big anxiety jumps between
adjacent items. For example if the third item causes
anxiety of 20 (on our 0 - 100 scale) and the fourth
item causes anxiety of 50, this is a big jump. Whenever you find a big jump add some additional items so
the change is much smaller. Remember our approach of
small steps. Using our 0 - 100 scale, it would be
good if there were not more than a 10-point difference
between adjacent items.

The next section gives some sample hierarchies.
After that you will start using your heirarchy to reduce your anxieties. Feel free to change your hierarchy over time. Add new items when you think of them.
Change the order of items when necessary. Change the
content of some of the situations so they are more
realistic or deal more directly with the problem. When
you start using your hierarchy, you will probably find
changes to be made.

SAMPLE HIERARCHIES
Fear of Spiders
1. hearing the word "spider"
2. seeing a cartoon of a spider
3. picture of a spider
4. close-up picture of a spider
5. small spider on a plant in the backyard
6. spider on its web in the garden
7. spider on the front porch
8. spider by the front door
9. spider just outside the window
10. spider in the garage
11. spider in corner of room by ceiling
12. spider on inside of window sill
13. spider moving across floor
14. spider running across table
15. spider crawling over your shoe
16. spider on your pants leg
17. spider on your shirt sleeve
18. spider walking over your bare foot
19. spider on back of your hand
20. letting spider crawl into your hand

Fear of Flying
1. planning a plane trip
2. morning of plane trip
3. loading luggage into car
4. driving to airport
5. parking at airport
6. entering airport terminal
7. checking in
8. boarding announcement
9. going to boarding gate
10. waiting to board
11. walking to plane
12. entering plane and finding seat
13. preparing for take-off
14. plane taxiing for take-off
15. plane take-off
16. plane in air

```
17.  landing gear going up
18.  plane in turbulent weather
```

Fear of Crowds

```
being in the following places:
1.   elevator with one other person
2.   large bus, 5 people
3.   small restaurant, one third full
4.   fairly empty shopping mall
5.   elevator with 3 other people
6.   large bus, one third full
7.   small restaurant, half full
8.   somewhat busy shopping mall
9.   elevator with 5 other people
10.  large bus, half full
11.  large restaurant, half full
12.  moderately busy shopping mall
13.  elevator, two thirds full
14.  large bus, two thirds full
15.  large restaurant, two thirds full
16.  busy shopping mall
17.  packed elevator
18.  large restaurant, full, busy, people waiting
19.  large bus, full, people standing
20.  packed shopping mall, mobs of people
```

Test Anxiety

```
1.   instructor announces test in 3 weeks
2.   instructor reminds of test in 2 weeks
3.   remember test coming up in one week
4.   two days before exam
5.   night before exam
6.   morning of exam
7.   going to exam room
8.   waiting for instructor
9.   instructor comes in with exams
10.  instructor passes out exams
11.  others beginning exam before you get yours
12.  looking over exam
13.  finding question you don't know answer for
14.  seeing others working faster than you
15.  others done and turning in exam
16.  only 10 minutes left to finish
17.  turn in exam with several questions unanswered
```

REDUCING YOUR FEARS: IMAGINATION

The procedures of this section are based on the approach of mental rehearsal discussed in Chapter 12. It would be useful for you to now go back and review that chapter.

Now let us start reducing anxiety. Find a place where you can be undisturbed and comfortable. Then do the procedures of the rest of this chapter at least 3 times a week. Begin the first day for at least 15 minutes and build up until you are doing it for at least 30 minutes each time.

Sit down or lie down, close your eyes, and relax as best you can. Now take the first situation from your anxiety hierarchy and imagine, as realistically as possible, being in that situation. Don't just see yourself in the situation like seeing yourself in a movie. Rather, live the situation. Be in it as best you can.

If while imagining being in this situation you start to feel anxious, then stop imagining and relax. You might wish to switch to imagining a pleasant situation. After you feel relaxed again return to imagining being in the first anxiety situation. If you feel anxiety again, stop imagining and relax. Continue to do this.

Eventually you will be able to imagine the whole first situation without feeling anxious. When you can do this twice in a row, move on to the second situation on the anxiety hierarchy. Work on this situation as you did the first: live the scene and relax when you feel anxious. When you can twice in a row imagine being in the second situation without feeling anxious, move on to the third situation on your hierarchy. Continue this procedure through the whole hierarchy.

On any one day you might spend all 30 minutes on one or two situations. Take your time. It would be better to move too slowly than too fast. If possible, end your daily session when you have imagined a situation without anxiety. When beginning a daily session, start with the item before the one you ended with on the session before. For example, if on one day you were working on item 5 at the end of the session, then the next session begin with item 4.

While working your way through your anxiety hierarchy, feel free to alter your hierarchy so you don't make any big jumps. Also alter any scenes to make them more realistic or easier to imagine.

Through this approach you will eventually be able to imagine any situation on your hierarchy without feeling anxious. This is a major accomplishment. You will have eliminated a lot of anxiety since it is your thoughts and images which trigger much of your anxiety. Your thinking in these areas will improve. You will find that the anxiety in the actual situations will be reduced. For example, if you eliminate feeling anxious when imagining seeing a snake, you will also reduce the anxiety you experience when seeing a snake in real life.

The carryover from imagined situations to real life situations is very useful and perhaps surprising. But now to finish the work we reduce what anxiety is still caused in the real world.

REDUCING YOUR FEARS: REAL WORLD
The last phase of fear reduction involves using the strategy you learned in the last section (fear reduction: imagination) and applying it to real world situations. For example, suppose you had a crowded shopping mall on your anxiety hierarchy. The proce- dure would consist of going to a mall when you expect it to be crowded. Then you would gradually enter the mall. If you feel anxious you would go out again and relax. Then you would go in again. You would continue this, perhaps over several days, until you could be in the crowded mall and not be overcome by anxiety.

In this real life practice, as in the imagination practice, you want to work slowly through your hierar- chy. Start with the first item on your hierarchy and go out and do that. When you can do that without anxi- ety, move on to the second item. And move through the whole hierarchy.

You may find that for some of your situations it is not practical or possible to go out and encounter them when you want. For example, the last item on the sample fear of flying hierarchy involves being on a plane in turbulent weather. Although you can do this readily in your imagination, you probably can't go out right now and get on a plane ride through turbulence. If you run across such impractical situations, just skip that item or look for a practical substitute. If many of your hierarchy situations are impractical in the real world, then put more emphasis on working with them in the imagination.

If you do the things in this chapter, you can re- duce or eliminate any fear you want. This is true no matter how strong the fear is or how long you have had it. But you must <u>do</u> something about it, be patient, and take small steps.

ADDITIONAL
The approach of this chapter goes very well with Chapter 7 (Calm and Relaxed Living). It would be worthwhile to reread that chapter.

If you have trouble staying motivated to do any of the things necessary, such as practicing relaxation or working through your hierarchy, then review the procedures of Chapter 8 (Getting Motivated).

Finally, remember that everything that was said in this chapter about anxiety can be applied to any unwanted negative emotion, such as anger or jealousy. You can keep an anger log, construct an anger hierarchy, imagine anger situations, and so forth.

SUGGESTED READING
Fensterheim and Baer survey several different ways to reduce fears. Rosen describes in detail an approach to fears similar to that of this chapter. Sutherland and associates use minimal hierarchies and encourage you to quickly confront the fear situations. If you follow this book, I would recommend you use their approach after you have worked your way through an imagined hierarchy as described in this chapter. The last book suggests a number of ways to overcome fear of flying.

Fensterheim H. & Baer, J. <u>Stop running scared!</u>
    Rawson, 1977. Dell paperback, 1978.
Rosen, G. <u>Don't be afraid: a program for overcoming
    your fears and phobias.</u> Prentice-Hall, 1976.
Sutherland, E. A. Amit, Z., and Weiner A. <u>Phobia
    free: How to fight your fears</u>. Stein & Day, 1977.
    Jove paperback, 1978.
Forgione, A. G. & Bauer, F. M. <u>Fearless flying: The
    complete program for relaxed air travel</u>. Houghton
    Mifflin, 1980.

CHAPTER SIXTEEN

EATING AND WEIGHT CONTROL

Being overweight is a common problem. 130 million Americans are too fat, with 80 million considered clinically obese. 30 million American children are already overweight.

Being overweight makes you more vulnerable to many health problems including high blood pressure, heart disease, respiratory problems, and diabetes. It also limits what clothes you can wear and in some cases requires the buying or ordering of special clothes. If you are overweight, it influences how others perceive you and act toward you. It can affect what jobs you are hired for and how you are evaluated at your work. Perhaps it shouldn't; but it does. Being overweight affects your social life and how attractive you are to others. It influences your sexual appeal. Being overweight will also affect how you feel about yourself, which then affects your moods, happiness, self-confidence, and how you act toward others.

So if you are overweight, losing weight and then controlling your weight will help you feel better, both physically and psychologically. In addition to better health you will also have less weight to carry around, will have more energy, and will be out of breath less often. You may also save money on food bills.

Many people lose weight by means of crash diets or reducing drugs. Although these may result in weight loss, most people who lose weight this way gain it back fairly quickly. Also many of the diet pills contain amphetamines, which can be addicting, may be physically harmful, and may lead to disturbances such as sleeplessness and feelings of agitation.

The most effective approach to weight loss and weight control is to change your eating habits. This chapter will help you learn how to get your eating under control which then will give you control over your weight. It is not a program in which you can never eat some food you like. Rather it is a program in which you learn self-control, so that sometimes you eat the food and other times you don't. You control your eating, so that you control the calories you take in, so that you control your weight.

113

A complete program in weight loss and weight control has 3 components: changing your eating habits (as discussed in this chapter), decreasing the calories you take in, and increasing exercise to use up calories. Decreasing calories and increasing exercise are discussed in Chapter 13 (Nutrition and Exercise), which should be read along with this chapter. But of the three components, changing your eating habits is the most important.

There are great individual differences in metabolism and physical limitations. Therefore it is often wise to check with your doctor about any particular diet, set of exercises, or weight loss program. For some people weight loss could be bad. This includes some pregnant or menopausal women, some older people, and some people with particular diseases such as Addison's disease or ulcerative colitis.

Now let us turn to exactly what you can do to control your eating.

OBSERVE YOUR EATING
It is necessary to learn when, how, and why you eat as you do. To learn this you need to observe your eating for a while. Review the general procedures of self-observation discussed in Chapter 3 (Know Yourself).

For at least one week, and preferably two weeks, keep written records of everything you eat and drink other than water. Your record sheet should have the following headings: date and time, situation, feelings and thoughts, what eaten or drunk, and approximate calories. Situation includes the place where you are and the people you are with. Feelings means whatever your mood is at the time you eat, such as happy, anxious, or tired. The thoughts you record should include such things as the thoughts you have about the situation, thoughts about your feelings, and thoughts about eating.

Learning to estimate the calories may take a little work at first, but it will be very useful in the long run as you learn to judge and control how many calories you eat. Books and charts of calories of common foods can be useful. Many foods have the calories listed on the label. And when preparing meals go out of your way to measure foods so that you can learn to visually judge amounts, such as how much a cup is.

After you have kept your records for a week or
two, carefully go over your records and see what you
can learn about your eating behavior. Do you tend to
overeat more in some situations than others? Are you
encouraged to eat or overeat by friends or family? Do
you eat when you are anxious or using certain drugs?
Is it the quantity, frequency, or nature (such as
sweets) of the foods that is the main problem? Are
there times of day when you are most likely to snack?
Continue to keep these types of records while carrying
out your weight loss program.

Make a graph on which you record your daily weight.
Weigh yourself at the same time each day. Put this
graph up in a very visible place, such as on the refrigerator door. Remember that daily weight change is
good to keep but is somewhat unreliable as a measure
of your progress, since many things can affect daily
weight changes. So keep daily weights but look at
changes from week to week as a better measure of progress. See Chapter 8 (Getting Motivated) for how the
graph can be part of a motivation-reward program.

SMALL STEPS
        Fast loss of weight will seldom hold and you will
generally gain it back. A better program is to try to
lose one or two pounds per week. If you did this for
a year,you would lose 50 to 100 pounds. Set a long
term goal for yourself, such as the loss of 40 pounds
at the average rate of one pound per week. Sometimes
a person's body metabolism adjusts to the decrease in
calories; the body then requires fewer calories for
the same basic activities and weight. If this happens
you may lose less weight each month even if you eat the
same. So put your emphasis on staying on your program
and be patient if your weight loss slows up or occasionally levels off for a short time. If you plan to
lose a lot of weight, say 40 pounds, you can let yourself hold at certain levels along the way. For example,
after you have lost 20 pounds, you might wish to hold
at this weight for a week or two before continuing on
with weight loss.

SETTING UP A PROGRAM
        The rest of this chapter contains suggestions for
changing eating habits which you can include in your
weight loss or weight control program. Design a program that suits you. But periodically re-evalaute and
change your program. You can't be expected to come up
with the best program for you right at first. Be sure

to include nutrition and exercise in your program.

It is very important that you include many motivation aids and rewards in your program (see Chapter 8, Getting Motivated), since you have to offset the pleasure of eating. You should have two types of rewards in your program. First you need daily rewards for carrying out your program, independent of any weight loss. Second you need bigger, long term rewards for losing a set amount of pounds, such as a reward when 10 pounds is lost and another when 20 pounds is lost.

FEELINGS

Do you eat when you are anxious, mad, depressed, or bored? Does eating reduce tension? Do you feed your emotions? Do you confuse anxiety and hunger? What do your written records of feelings tell you?

If feelings are a major cause of eating, then you want to deal with your feelings first. If you eat when bored, then find other things to do instead of eating. If you eat when you are upset, then review the following previous chapters: Relaxing Body and Mind (Chapter 6), Calm and Relaxed Living (Chapter 7), and Fears (Chapter 15).

THOUGHTS

What do your written records tell you about what you think before and during eating? Do some of your thoughts cause feelings which lead to overeating? Do some of your thoughts encourage or justify overeating? Examples of such thoughts are: I can never lose weight. I'll always be overweight. I'll start a new diet tomorrow. I have already eaten too much so one more piece won't hurt. I can't sleep so I'll have something to eat. Someone with my bone structure can't lose much weight. It is important to clean my plate. I should eat more to please.... I can't help being overweight; it is due to....

Review Chapter 11 (What Do You Think) for ways to evaluate and change thinking which leads to or supports overeating.

REMOVE AND AVOID

From your general observing of your eating and from your written records note those situations in which it is more probable that you will overeat and/or eat something undesirable. Is it possible to avoid some of these situations for a while until you get your

eating under more control? Are there some cues that
trigger eating which you can remove, for good or at
least for a while? Review the first part of Chapter
5 (Change of Scene) about removing and avoiding such
cues and situations. Next are some suggestions of
remove and avoid.

Remove all snacks, such as candy and pretzels,
from your desk, purse, and car. Remove any such food
that is sitting out in plain view in your home or office. Remove from your home all foods that are very
tempting, particularly if they are high in calories.
If you must occasionally have these foods, do it outside your home. Remove all prepared snacks. If you
must have snacks, then have snacks that require some
preparation. Rewrap food in smaller portions that
you only take one at a time. Keep food in containers
you can't see through and unscrew the bulb in your
refrigerator so you don't see the food as well. Remove
some of the hunger cues by drinking a large glass of
water when hungry and before a meal.

Get out of your kitchen or even out of your house
if you feel very tempted to eat. Avoid the kitchen
as much as possible. If you nibble when fixing meals,
chew sugarless gum when preparing meals and/or fix the
meal when not hungry, such as preparing dinner right
after you have had lunch. Rearrange your cupboards and
refrigerator so problem foods are more out of sight and
out of reach. Wrap and seal foods very tightly. Avoid
giving yourself shots of energy with candy and sugar;
this is unhealthy and addicting. Avoid drinking alcohol while eating; it may increase your appetite and/or
dull your thinking about your weight control program.
Alcoholic drinks are also often very high in calories.

Avoid food and candy machines and/or don't have
the change to use them. Avoid places like bakeries by
taking different routes, at least the other side of
the street. Avoid doing grocery shopping on an empty
stomach. Learn to prepare and use a shopping list;don't
buy extra food. Prepare your shopping list when you are
not hungry. If you don't buy it, you can't eat it!

RESTRICT
Most people who have a problem with weight control
tend to eat in many situations, such as when reading,
watching television, talking on the phone, and entertaining guests. This causes these situations to become
associated with eating so that when in the situation,

you tend to eat. If you eat when watching television, after a while watching television will cue eating.

In addition these are situations in which you don't pay full attention to eating. Much of the eating is automatic and unconscious. If you are overweight and enjoy eating, why eat at times when you don't give it full attention and get full pleasure?

For these reasons it is very useful if you restrict all your eating, meals and snacks, to one place at specific times. Pick a place, such as a particular chair at a particular place at the table, and do all of your eating there. Sit down; never eat on the run. Develop a routine for eating. Have your meals at the same time each day and do not eat at other times. If you must have snacks, have them at the same time each day. Pick eating times which best fit your schedule and occur when you are most hungry. See your records for such possible times.

If you have too much trouble with this restricting, then use a gradual approach (small steps). Start your restricting with those times and situations which are easiest for you to eliminate. Then move on to the harder times and situations. Gradually restrict your eating more and more to one place and specific times.

Develop alternative things you can do in place of snacking and overeating. If you have an urge for a snack, do something else, such as read, take a walk, make a phone call, do a puzzle, sew or knit, write a letter, or do some gardening. You might plan activities for times of the day when it is most difficult to avoid eating. You might also wish to reward yourself for doing some of these things instead of eating.

MEALS

Learn to make a variety of low calorie meals. Get a cookbook with low calorie recipes. Learn how to add more variety to all your recipes and meals with various flavorings and spices. Make the meal as attractive as possible. Set an attractice table. Make the meal look like more by using smaller plates and/or spreading it out on the plate. Restrict how much you eat by planning the meal ahead and dishing out the whole meal on the plate, rather than continually helping yourself from a serving dish. Begin the meal with bulky and chewy foods.

118

Serve the meal in such a way it helps slow down eating. For example, serve food hot and/or serve more foods that take longer to eat, such as soup. Use teaspoons instead of soup spoons and/or eat more with chop sticks. Use utensils for everything you eat, including such things as sandwiches.

At the beginning of a meal sit for a few minutes before eating. Practice self-control. Don't eat it if you don't need to. Eat slowly! It takes some time for your stomach to signal your brain about how much you have eaten. So if you slow down you will eat less. You might set a minimum time to eat your meal. Periodically during the meal take a break for 2 minutes during which you don't eat. Gradually increase these breaks to 5 minutes. If you must have dessert, wait at least 20 minutes from the end of the rest of the meal.

Take small bites and chew very thoroughly. Be sure to set down your utensils while chewing.

Pay full attention to your eating. Minimize doing other things, such as talking and thinking, while eating. Put your full attention on all of the details of eating while you eat slowly. Notice in detail how the food looks, smells, and feels as you prepare it to eat and bring it toward your mouth. Notice in detail how the food smells, tastes, and feels as you chew and swallow it. If you put your full attention on eating, you will have more pleasure eating than before, when you ate more but much of the eating was automatic and unconscious. This practice will also be useful for your concentration, quieting your mind, and/or meditation and mindfulness.

Eat your favorite food on the plate first rather than saving it for last. If you save it for last, you will probably eat all of it even if you are pretty full; while if less desirable foods are last, you might stop eating sooner.

Don't start your program by trying to eliminate your favorite foods. Start by cutting back on the eating of less desirable foods and gradually build up to your favorites.

Don't eat to avoid waste. Don't help others finish their meals. Don't eat something because there is not enough to save or you don't want to throw food away.

119

Your health is more important than waste. Your waist is more important than your waste. Find other things to do with left-over food other than eating it now.

Stop eating before you are full. Then immediately remove the food from the table or leave the table. Practice leaving some food on your plate at the end of a meal. Start by leaving some of the least desirable food and then gradually work up to leaving some of the most desirable food.

Sit down. Slow down. Cut down.

DESIRES

You may need to work on your general desire for food. If so, see the last half of Chapter 10 (Out of Habit) for the section on desires, including disrupting desires, overloading procedures, and the use of unpleasant associations.

SUPPORT FROM OTHERS

It is common for other people to encourage your overeating or even sabotage your attempts to lose weight. There are many possible reasons for this. For example, a mother may encourage her child to eat more because she thinks it is healthier. A wife may want her husband to eat a lot because meals are an important part of their relationship or time together. A man may find his wife more attractive when she is plump. Or a man may want his wife fat so she will be less attractive to other men.

Notice to what extent other people encourage you to overeat and/or do or say things that slow up your weight control program. When you find other people working against you in one of these ways, talk with them and find out their reasons for what they are doing. Try to get them to co-operate with you in your program. In some cases, such as a spouse who continually sabotages your programs for reasons he or she won't discuss, you both may need to see a professional counselor.

Don't let yourself be forced into overeating. You make the decisions on what you eat. Sample different foods and compliment the person who prepared them, but don't overeat to flatter. Be polite, but don't be pushed. Similarly, you don't have to eat cookies or cake because someone gave them to you for your home. You can appreciate the gift; but you don't have to eat it. Health is more important than a false sense of social responsibility.

On the other hand, do what you can to get other people to help and support your weight program, as is discussed in the last of Chapter 5 (Change of Scene). Get others to help you with different parts of your program and praise your work and improvement.

SOCIAL EATING
Many people have trouble with eating and weight control because food is tied into many social events and aspects of entertaining. But this need not be.

You can be a good host, entertaining people at your home, without serving food. Or if you do serve food, you can have the guests take extra food, such as left-over desserts, with them. If you have a party with snacks, fix some or many low calorie snacks,which many of your guests might appreciate. You might also fix food which is good but not your favorites. Also put all food in one area and avoid this area.

If you are out to eat, eat some low calorie food before going. If you are going to a friend's house, tell him or her well in advance that you are on a diet and what you would like to avoid. If you go to a res-taurant, buy things separately (a la carte) rather than a complete meal, ask about food substitutes, and ask the waiter not to bring problem foods such as bread. When you are out to eat, enjoy what you choose to eat. Then rather than eating more, enjoy the people and the setting.

If you feel that you need some excuses for not eating more, then practice these excuses in advance. While at home use mental rehearsal, as described in Chapter 12, to imagine the social situation you will later be in. Then in your imagination practice your excuses to different situations that may arise. Here are some sample excuses: I just ate dinner and can't eat any more right now. I can't eat this right now, but will save it for later when I can really enjoy it. I can't eat any more; I filled up on your wonderful.... No, thank you, I am saving room for....

LONG TERM MAINTENANCE
You can use the information in this chapter to put together a program that will work for you and let you lose whatever weight you want and then control your weight. Be patient; it will take a little time and

some work to find the program that is just right for you. Then when you have a pretty good program, stay with it. Be patient and consistent.

Some parts of the program are temporary, such as some of the avoiding procedures. These can be slowly phased out after your eating is under control. But many parts of the program will lead to long term habits that will be with you for as long as you want. You will learn control and skills you don't now have.

Even after you have reached the goals of your program, continue to check your weight at least weekly and re-evaluate how you are doing and what you should do next. Also every now and then keep detailed records of your eating as described at the beginning of this chapter. This will help you stay in touch with your eating habits and your body.

The condition of your body is up to you. What are you going to do now?

SUGGESTED READING
The following are good books on weight loss,weight control, and related topics such as diet and exercise. The different books emphasize different things and are written in different ways. Therefore if weight loss and control is of particular interest to you, you would profit by reading one or more of these books.

Amit, Z. & Sutherland, E. G. Stay slim for good.
    Charter paperback, 1978.
Fanburg, W. H. & Snyder, B. M. How to be a winner at
    the weight loss game. Simon & Schuster, 1975.
    Ballantine paperback, 1976.
Jeffrey, D. B. & Katz, R. C. Take it off and keep it
    off, Prentice-Hall, 1977.
Jordan. H. A. et al. Eating is okay. Rawson, 1976.
    Signet paperback, 1978.
Mahoney, M. J. & Mahoney, K. Permanent weight control.
    Norton, 1976.
Stuart, R. B. Act thin, stay thin. Norton, 1978.
    Jove paperback, 1983.

CHAPTER SEVENTEEN

SMOKING

Smoking tobacco is one of the major health problems in the United States. Over 40% of everyone in
the U.S. smokes. It is a habit which is psychologically
addicting and often physically addicting. This chapter
will show you how to get free from this dangerous habit
and how to stop smoking. The focus of the chapter is on
smoking tobacco cigarettes, but the approach described
also applies to smoking cigars and pipes and the smoking of marijuana.

HOW DID YOU BEGIN?
Why do peole begin smoking? Why would a person
choose to draw hot smoke into his lungs? For most
people it is unpleasant at first; the body does not
like it. Most people have to learn to like and need
cigarettes. Why would they do that?

In most cases people begin smoking for social reasons. Some start because their friends smoke and they
wish to be part of the group. Others take up smoking
to appear older or more sophisticated. An unfortunate
aspect of the women's liberation movement was that more
women began smoking; and becoming addicted is the opposite of becoming liberated. Children begin smoking
at early ages, 10 years old not being uncommon. Children and teenagers are usually influenced by their
friends to smoke and/or they imitate their parents who
smoke. The fact that smoking is often not allowed or
illegal usually just makes it more desirable and exciting to smoke.

BUT WHY CONTINUE?
But why do people continue to smoke, particularly
if they can see how it hurts them? Here the reasons
are many. Some people continue to smoke for social
reasons. They are still concerned with maintaining
some image or fitting in with their friends who smoke.
For some people smoking reduces anxiety and they smoke
when nervous or uptight. For others it gives them
something to do with their hands. Some people learn
to like the taste and/or the sensations of smoking.

For most smokers smoking becomes associated with
many of the situations and activities of their lives.
It becomes natural to have a cigarette after a meal,

with a cocktail, when talking on the phone, and many other times. This is part of what makes smoking such a strong habit; it gets tied into much of a person's life.

For most smokers smoking is a habit, an addiction. They can not stop smoking except for a short period of time, even if they think or say they can. But the main reason they can't stop is that they don't know how. This chapter will provide you with proven ways that will work for you.

It may be hard to stop, particularly if you have been smoking 2 to 3 packs a day for many years. But you can do it. Then when you have stopped, you have accomplished something you deserve to take great pride in. Here is a chance to do something significant with your life.

A STOP SMOKING PROGRAM

It is time now for you to get on with your own program to stop smoking. This chapter suggests many things to do. Pick out those suggestions that make sense to you; but the more you include, the better. Then get started with your program. Be prepared to revise your program as you see how to make it better for you. If you stay with it you can do it. It is important that you reward yourself for carrying out your program; so review Chapter 8 (Getting Motivated) and include ways to increase motivation. One way to get more motivated is to make a list of reasons for stopping.

REASONS TO STOP

Make a list of reasons for quitting smoking, reasons that are meaningful to you. Some possible reasons are given below. Post this list in a very visible place and read through the list every day. Add to the list as you think of new reasons. After you have done this for a few weeks, pick 4 or 5 of the reasons that are the most important to you and put these on a list for daily review. Save the longer list and get it out occasionally and go through it. Now here are some good reasons to stop smoking:

Smoking is terrible to your health. Smokers get more illnesses, miss more work, spend more days in the hospital, have more surgery, and die earlier than non-smokers. Smokers are 10-50 times more likely to die of lung cancer, the type of cancer that causes the most

deaths. Smokers are also more vulnerable to cancers
of the mouth, larynx, esophagus, and bladder. Smoking
often leads to heart disease, bronchitis, and emphy-
sema. Smoking can result in more colds, trouble sleeping, and a greater chance of an unsuccessful pregnancy.
Smoking can lead to decreased stamina and shortness of
breath. Smoking can cause bad breath, a hacking cough,
waking up with a coated tongue, and stained teeth and
fingers. Smoking can decrease your senses of taste
and smell. On the positive side, if you quit smoking,
your body can probably repair itself and you will eventually be as healthy as if you had never smoked!

Smokers live in a self-created smog. The smell
of smoke gets into their clothes and hair. Their homes
and cars smell. They often leave vile-smelling
ashtrays about. Smokers drop ashes all about and sometimes burn holes in papers, clothes, and furniture.
Many smokers have set fire to their bed and/or house.
Some smokers spend a lot of time and concern checking
to see if they have left a cigarette lit somewhere.

Smoking can hurt others around you who are forced
to breathe your smoke. For example, children of
smokers are more susceptible to respiratory diseases
than children of non-smokers. Some people don't like
to be around smokers. They don't like the smoke and
don't want it on their clothes and person. Smoking
while people are eating can foul up their tastes. Your
smoking can be a bad example to your children and other
people. If you are a smoker, you are partially responsible if your children become smokers, even if you tell
them not to.

Smoking costs a lot of money. Consider how much
you spend for cigarettes, lighters, ashtrays, pipes,
humidors, etc. Stop now and figure out about how much
you spend a year on smoking. For example, if you smoke
just one pack of cigarettes a day, that is 365 packs
a year. How much is that at the current cost per pack?
One thing you might do as you stop smoking is put aside
the money you save each day or week into a fund for
something special. You might put this money in a glass
jar and watch it mount up. Another way you might save
money is on your insurance. Some insurance companies
give discounts to non-smokers (auto, home, life) because they are healthier and less of a risk.

Smoking is an addiction that can lead to strange
behaviors. A smoker out of cigarettes may drive around

125

at night looking for a place that is open and sells cigarettes, or he may smoke butts he finds in ashtrays. A smoker may leave a movie or concert in the middle because he craves cigarettes. Thoughts and concerns about cigarettes may dominate a smoker's mind so he can not fully enjoy other things.

So ask yourself which is stronger: You or a cigarette? You or the multimillion dollar attack by the cigarette manufacturers? You or the social pressure from others? Stopping smoking can lead to great freedom.

EXCUSES

Most smokers are really good at coming up with excuses for why they can not quit right now and/or why smoking is not as harmful for them as others. Be alert for any of your excuses and don't fall for them! Smoking is bad for you and you can quit now.

Some smokers argue they can't quit because they are too old, they have been smoking too long, or they are physiologically addicted. This is nonsense. Anyone can quit if he is willing to work at it.

Many smokers argue that the pleasure they get from smoking is worth any disadvantages. But this is the type of justification that addicts of all kinds use. And it doesn't hold up. First of all, the world is filled with more sources of pleasure than you could ever enjoy, and many are much better than smoking. So you can have just as much, or more, pleasure in life without smoking. Also your life will become more pleasurable when you quit, for many reasons including improved health, better senses of smell and taste, and greater overall freedom.

Many smokers argue they could quit any time they wanted to, but now is not the time because.... This is a standard delaying tactic used by addicts. If you can quit, then do it now! Perhaps you are avoiding quitting because you are afraid to find out you are more caught by cigarettes than you want to believe. Don't worry; this chapter shows you how to quit.

Some people are concerned about stopping smoking because they might gain weight. If this happens it will probably just be a few temporary pounds. If you weigh yourself daily beginning a week before you stop smoking, you will probably find that any weight gain

due to quitting smoking is pretty small. First stop
smoking and then lose any weight you wish. The skills
you learn from stopping smoking will help you with any
weight loss. (See the previous chapter on weight loss.)

OBSERVE YOUR SMOKING
     It is very important to spend some time observing
your smoking and keeping written records about when and
how you smoke. It would be useful here to review Chapter 3 (Know Yourself).

     You should keep written records of your smoking,
as described below, for one to two weeks before beginning your program to stop. These records will help you
know what to emphasize in your program. In addition,
make a graph on which you put the number of cigarettes
smoked each day. Continue keeping the graph and written records during the time you are carrying out your
program to stop. They will help you watch your progress
and spot problem areas. The graph can also be a part
of your program to reward yourself (see Chapter 8, Getting Motivated).

     Your written records should have the following
headings: Date and Time, Situation, Feelings, and
Thoughts. Under "Date and Time" you write when you
smoke each time. Under "Situation" you briefly describe the situation you are in at the time, including
where you are, who is there, and what is happening.
Under "Feelings" you put how you felt before smoking,
such as anxious or excited. Under "Thoughts" write
any thoughts you had about smoking or thoughts about
your feelings just before you began to smoke.

     Carry a piece of paper or notebook with you so
that you can record every time you smoke, including
when you get a cigarette from someone else. A records
paper wrapped around your pack of cigarettes is one
way to do this. Try to record your information as
soon as possible. One good method is to record your
information before lighting the cigarette. This may
cause you not to smoke sometimes. After you have kept
such records for a week or so, look carefully at them
to learn more about when and why you smoke. Don't
continue further in this chapter until you have kept
records for at least a week.

FEELINGS AND THOUGHTS
     Look at what you listed under Feelings in your
records. Do you often smoke when you are nervous,

127

anxious, angry, irritable, or depressed? If so, then
dealing with these feelings should be a part of your
stop smoking program. If such feelings are the major
reason you smoke, then you must work with the feelings
first! See Chapter 6 (Relaxing Body and Mind), Chapter
7 (Calm and Relaxed Living) and Chapter 15 (Fears).

Next look at the thoughts you have before smoking,
as listed in your records. Do some of your thoughts
produce or increase feelings that lead to smoking? Are
some of your thoughts excuses or justifications for
smoking? If your thoughts do anything like this, review Chapter 11 (What Do You Think?) for ways to change
your thoughts.

REMOVE, AVOID, RESTRICT

From your written records and from observing your
smoking, make a list of situations and cues around
which you tend to smoke. Think of ways to remove or
avoid these situations and cues until your smoking is
decreased. Review the techniques of removing and
avoiding at the beginning of Chapter 5 (Change of Scene).

Remove. Get rid of all extra cigarettes. Do not
buy a new pack until you have used up the old. Do not
stockpile cigarettes. When ready to quit, get rid of
all cigarettes anywhere. Also get all ashtrays,
matches, lighters, and other smoking-related objects
out of sight and hard to get to. Take the ashtray out
of your car.

Avoid. During the first few weeks of your program
avoid as many situations as you can in which you would
usually smoke (see your written records for some of
these situations). Thus you might avoid coffee breaks
with others, card games, or parties. Go to places
where you seldom or never smoke, such as movies, con-
certs, library, church, or homes of non-smoking friends.
Have a list of non-smoking activities to do when you
desire to smoke, activities such as exercising or
showering. During the first few days of non-smoking
you may wish to schedule many such activities during
the day.

Restrict. Like overeating, a major problem with
smoking is that people do it with so many activities,
such as reading, watching television, and talking with
others. These activities then become associated with
smoking so that when doing one of them you tend to
smoke. You turn on the television and light up a

cigarette. So until you are ready to totally stop
smoking it is helpful to restrict your smoking. When
you smoke don't do anything else. Don't socialize or
read; just smoke. When at home restrict all your smoking to one place, such as a chair in the basement or
garage. When you must smoke, go to that chair and
smoke. Don't do anything else while sitting and smoking.
This restricting will weaken the habit and make it
easier eventually to totally quit.

MAKE SMOKING A COMMOTION

Since it is very easy to smoke, most smokers smoke
more than they want or need to. Thus a good way of reducing the smoking habit is to make it a commotion to
smoke. One way is to put the cigarettes and matches in
out-of-the-way places. The cigarettes might be on the
top shelf of a cabinet that you must stand on a chair
to get to; the matches might be in a box in the garage.
Then when you want to smoke, get just one cigarette
and return the cigarettes and matches to their out-of-
the-way places.

When going out you might wrap up your cigarette
pack in paper and string that you have to undo and rewrap for every cigarette. Or you might tape a cigarette
to your leg so you have to take off some clothes to get
it.

Another way to make smoking a commotion is to have
a ritual you must go through in order to smoke. For
example, when you have the desire to smoke force yourself to wait 3 minutes. Then during this time try to
do something else and not think about smoking. This
will help break the habit.

MAKE SMOKING LESS DESIRABLE

To further weaken the smoking habit you may wish
to make smoking less pleasant. You might smoke brands
you don't like or cigarettes you let get stale. The
last half of Chapter 10 (Out of Habit) discusses dealing with desires, such as the desire to smoke. Included in this discussion is the technique of "unpleasant associations" which is a useful way to make
smoking less desirable.

ALTERNATIVES FOR HANDS AND MOUTH

For many smokers part of the support of their
smoking is that it gives them something to do with
their hands and/or something to have in their mouths.
Is this true for you? If it is, then when you start

decreasing your smoking it may be useful to have other
things to do with your hands and mouth. For your hands
you might get a nice feeling stone, a key chain, or
worry beads to handle. Part of the time you might use
your hands for painting or knitting. Substitutes for
your mouth might include gum, lifesavers, cloves,
carrot sticks, toothpicks, or wooden matches with the
heads cut off.

These are only temporary measures while you quit
smoking. Later these can be phased out. If you have
a need for something to do with your hands because you
are nervous see Chapters 5 & 6 for relaxing and being
more calm. Chapter 10 shows you how to reduce nervous
habits, such as habits involving your hands and mouth.

QUITTING
Now it's time for you to put all this together in
a program which will lead to your becoming a non-
smoker. Let us review a few things. First you must
be ready and motivated to stop. The list of reasons
helps here. You also need to be careful you don't fall
for any excuses for why you can't or shouldn't quit.
Then you need to observe your smoking and keep written
records so you know what needs to be emphasized in a
program that will work for you. Some people need to
emphasize reducing feelings that lead to smoking. Others
need to work more on what they think about smoking. All
of these things should be done before the actual quitting of smoking.

Now quitting itself can be approached in one of
two ways: gradual and cold turkey. In the gradual approach you slowly cut down how much you smoke until
you have stopped smoking. This approach follows our
rule of taking small steps. The cold turkey approach
involves totally stopping all at once. You can also
combine these by gradually decreasing to some level,
say 10 or 5 cigarettes a day, and then quitting totally.
You should choose the approach that you think will work
best for you. If you are not sure, use the gradual
approach.

Depending on which approach you take determines
how you use some of the procedures discussed earlier:
remove, avoid, restrict, making smoking a commotion,
making smoking less desirable, and alternatives for
hands and mouth. In the gradual approach you would
gradually build these in as you reduce smoking. In the
cold turkey approach you would do some of them to weaken

the smoking habit and then do the rest when you quit for good. Whatever approach you take be sure to build in rewards for yourself both for carrying out the various steps in your program and for reducing and quitting smoking (see Chapter 8, Getting Motivated).

Cold turkey. If you decide to go cold turkey, be sure you are ready. Pick a day to quit when it will be easier than other days, a day when you won't have to be in many situations that lead you to smoke, a day with few pressures, a day with other things to do. You might quit when an illness makes smoking unpleasant or impossible. Or you might quit on a day which has some significance to you such as the day after your birthday (Quitting on your birthday could be too hard and interfere with your birthday).

Gradual. There are many ways to gradually cut back on smoking. The simplest is to gradually reduce the number of cigarettes you allow yourself each day. Here are three other ways that often work better.

One way involves increasing the time between cigarettes. Start by gradually putting off the time of day when you have the first cigarette. Each day have your first cigarette 15 to 30 minutes later than the day before. Next gradually increase the amount of time between cigarettes. Timers and wrist alarms can be useful here.

The second way involves increasing the times of day during which you don't smoke. From your written records find the times of day in which you smoke the least. Then don't smoke at all during these times and gradually let these times get longer and longer each day. Also gradually add other non-smoking times into your day and increase them.

The third way to gradually decrease is to slowly eliminate the situations in which you smoke. Using your written records as a guide, make a rank order of the situations in which you want or need to smoke. This is a list with the top of the list being the situation you most smoke in and the bottom being the situation you least need to smoke. Then start by eliminating smoking in the situation at the bottom of your list and slowly work your way up the list, eliminating smoking in situation after situation.

While reducing how much you smoke, it is also use-

131

ful to reduce the inhaling of tar and nicotine. Don't smoke cigarettes all the way, as you get the most tar and nicotine in the last of the cigarette. Consider switching to cigarettes which have less and less tar and nicotine. Reduce inhaling. Take short drags or just puff. Or switch to big cigars you don't inhale.

Whether you use gradual approaches, cold turkey, or some combination, soon you will be a non-smoker. This is an accomplishment to be proud of. After you quit keep many parts of your program going for a while and then gradually phase off them. For example, you may wish to continue working with your feelings or avoiding some smoking situations. For a few weeks continue to record each day of non-smoking and the amount of money saved.

STAYING A NON-SMOKER
Now that you have stopped smoking you have done something very good for your body and mind. Just don't start again for any reason! Don't worry about never smoking again; only be concerned about not smoking the next cigarette. You'll have no trouble if you just take things a day at a time. Occasionally get out your list of reasons for stopping and review the advantages of being a non-smoker.

A trap for many ex-smokers is that at some time they come up with reasons for smoking again. It is very important that you know about this trap in advance and decide now that no matter what the reason you don't start smoking. You need to realize this now because when the time comes you may fall for the reason. Know in advance that there is no good reason; it is only your mind setting a trap.

Here are two common "reasons" ex-smokers often fall for. The first is that because of problems in the person's life smoking is somehow justified. The person tells himself that somehow smoking will help him cope with his problems and the disadvantages of smoking are minor compared to these other problems. This is nonsense. There are better ways of dealing with the problems and starting smoking just adds another problem.

The second common trap is for the ex-smoker to tell himself that now that he has stopped he can have an occasional cigarette every now and then. After all, one every week or so can't hurt. Well, the occasional cigarette becomes more and more frequent surprisingly

132

fast. Soon the person is back smoking as much as before he quit. It is best not to smoke at all.

If, however, for whatever reasons you do start again, don't get discouraged or believe you can not stop. Learn from your mistakes, revise your program, and get on with becoming a non-smoker. You are probably somewhat healthier from the time you did stop and you certainly learned things that will help you stop again.

You can become and remain a non-smoker. The choice is yours. What are you going to do now?

SUGGESTED READING

Danaher, B. G. & Lichtenstein, E. Become an ex-smoker. Prentice-Hall, 1978.

Halper, M. S. How to stop smoking. Holt, Rinehart and Winston, 1981

Pomerleau, O. F. & Pomerleau, C. S. Break the smoking habit. Research Press, 1977.

CHAPTER EIGHTEEN

ALCOHOL

Drinking too much alcohol is one of the major
health problems in the United States and one of the
major causes of death. There are about 10 million
alcoholics in the U.S. and the average life span of
alcoholics is 12 years less than for non-alcoholics.
A person who drinks four or more drinks a day, as compared to the non-drinker, is twice as likely to die of
heart disease, twice as likely to die of cancer, and
twelve times as likely to get cirrhosis of the liver.
Drinking while pregnant can lead to infant death or
birth defects. Drinking can lead to nausea, hangovers,
and sexual problems such as impotence. Alcohol has a
surprising number of calories, a problem for people
concerned about their weight. One ounce of alcohol has
about 100 calories and a bottle of beer can contain 160
calories. In varying degrees drinkers can become physiologically addicted to alcohol as their bodies adjust
to the alcohol. This can lead to withdrawal symptoms
such as headaches and tension which can lead to con-
vulsions and hallucinations. (If you experience any of
these physiological effects, see a doctor.)

Alcohol is a factor in one-third of all murders
and other violent crimes in the U.S. One-half of all
fatal traffic accidents involve a drinking driver.
Drinking problems often lead to problems with family,
friends and work. It can lead to loss of control, such
as passing out at a party, vomiting at a nightclub, or
falling down. Drinking can make people unpleasant to
be with, as when they get too depressed, aggressive,
loud, or foolish. People can spend a lot of money on
alcohol, particularly buying mixed drinks in bars.

Given all these disadvantages, why do so many
people drink alcohol? For some people alcohol helps
reduce anxiety or boredom. It gives them temporary
escape from some of their problems. Most drinkers
began drinking and continue drinking for social reasons.
Drinking is an important part of many parties and other
social events. People are often encouraged and rewarded
by others for drinking and perhaps for getting drunk.
Drinking is often an excuse for people to act unin-
hibited and get away with things they would not ordinarily do or say. Many men consider drinking a lot to
be a sign of manhood. Thus it is often difficult for

135

a man to admit to himself or others he has a drinking problem.

It can be seen that the immediate effects of drinking are often pleasurable, such as a reduction in anxiety and social approval of friends. While the negative aspects of drinking, such as health and family problems, are more long range. This is a common trap of many addictions, including eating, drinking, and smoking too much. For a person's behavior is often more influenced by immediate effects than long term effects. Self-control often involves getting free from this trap so that long term effects have an equal or greater influence.

The concern of this chapter is not whether you drink alcohol or not; that is your decision. The concern here is whether you have a problem with drinking, if drinking has become a habit out of control, if you drink more than you wish or should. A glass of wine with dinner or a couple of drinks at a party is one thing; but a habit out of control that hurts your body, mind, and life is another thing.

DO YOU HAVE A DRINKING PROBLEM?
The first thing is that you must be totally honest with yourself about whether you have a drinking problem. Here are some questions to ask yourself: Would you have trouble going for a week without having a drink? Do you often need a drink to do something or go somewhere? Do you drink early in the day? Do you often drink alone? Do you ever drive while drunk? Have you had any contacts with the law due to drinking? Do you ever go to work intoxicated? Do you drink before going to a place where you will drink much more? Do you do things while drunk you would not do otherwise? Does your drinking have any negative effects on your family, friends, or work? If you answered yes to some of these questions, you may have a drinking problem or the beginning of a problem.

REDUCING DRINKING
The rest of this chapter contains suggestions for what you might put into your program to reduce your drinking. It is necessary for you to develop a program that is geared for you. Revise your program as you see ways to improve it, and stay with it until your drinking is under control. Be sure to give a strong emphasis to motivation and reward in your program (see Chapter 8, Getting Motivated). Also it would

136

be useful to read the two previous chapters on eating and smoking, as they should give you some ideas you can apply to drinking.

Some people with a drinking problem can learn controlled drinking. They can learn to have a drink or two and stop. This is often possible if the drinking problem is not yet too serious. However, many other people with drinking problems must totally stop drinking. If they have even a drink or two it will probably lead back to problem drinking. Even if you are sure you can learn controlled drinking, it would be best for you to totally stop for a while and not do any drinking until you straighten out other problems in your life.

For some of you it would be best to seek professional help (see Chapter 28, Choosing a Counselor). The drinking problem may be too difficult for you to handle yourself. Or you may need help with problems related to your drinking, such as problems with your marriage or work. Don't be embarrassed about seeking help; it is often the best thing to do.

Now let us consider what you can do for yourself.

REASONS TO DECREASE DRINKING
To help with your motivation it is useful to make a list of reasons to decrease drinking, reasons that are important to you. The material at the beginning of this chapter may suggest some reasons. After you have made your list, post it in a place you see often. Then read through the list at least once a day. Add new reasons to the list as you think of them.

After doing this for a few weeks, pick 4 or 5 of your best reasons and post this list for your daily review. Save your larger list and every now and then get it out and go through it.

OBSERVE YOUR DINKING
It is very important that you practice objectively observing when and where you drink, why you drink, and how much you drink. This is the first step in self-control of drinking. It would be good here to review Chapter 3 (Know Yourself).

It is easy for anyone to overlook important aspects of his drinking and/or fool himself about what he really does. Therefore it is important to keep written records

137

for two weeks before beginning your program to decrease drinking and to continue these written records while carrying out the program.

Your written records should have the following headings: Date & Time, Situation, Feelings, Desire, Thoughts, What Drunk, and Reactions of Others. Under "Situation" write where you are, who is there, and what is going on. Under "Feelings" note how you felt before drinking, such as anxious, angry, bored, or excited. For "Desire" put a number from 1 to 5 that indicates how strong your desire to drink was: 1 means you really needed a drink; 2 means you needed a drink but could have let it go; 3 is you wanted a drink but didn't need it; 4 means the drink was desirable but not necessary; and 5 is for when there was some question about whether or not you would have the drink. Under "Thoughts" record any thoughts you had before and during drinking which were related to your feelings, desires, or drinking. In the "What Drunk" column list what types of drinks you had and how much, such as number of bottles of beer or ounces of whiskey. Learn to estimate ounces by pouring drinking glasses of water into a measuring cup. For "Reactions of Others" note how the people around you reacted to your drinking. Did they encourage your drinking? Did they discourage you?

Carry your record sheet or record notebook with you. Then record the above information as soon as possible after each time you did some drinking. This will be very useful information for your program. Keep these records for at least two weeks before continuing further in this chapter.

RELATED PROBLEMS
     Look over your records and think about why you drink. Is a major reason you drink because of difficulties in some area of your life, like marriage problems, job dissatisfaction, or interpersonal problems. If so, then these problems need to be dealt with first or at the same time.

From the "Feelings" column in your records and from what you know about yourself, to what extent do you drink to change your feelings? Do you drink because you are anxious, angry, or bored? If so, it is important that you learn other ways to handle your feelings. Chapter 6 (Relaxing Body and Mind) and Chapter 7 (Calm and Relaxed Living) should be useful here. Chapter 15 (Fears) shows you how to deal with situations

138

that cause anxiety. The same approach can be used for
other unwanted feelings, such as anger or jealousy.

THOUGHTS

Look at the "Thoughts" column of your records.
What types of thoughts do you have before and during
drinking? Do some of these thoughts cause or increase
feelings that lead to drinking? Do some of the thoughts
encourage, justify, or excuse drinking? If your
thoughts do any of these things or anything else undesirable, then review Chapter 11 (What Do You Think)
for ways to evaluate and change thoughts.

REMOVE AND AVOID

It is useful to you to come to understand the
times, situations, and cues that lead to or are associated with your drinking. You can learn about these
from your written records and from generally observing
your drinking patterns. From the "Date & Time" column
of your records see if there are certain days of the
week and times of day when you drink the most. From
the "Situation" column see if you do most of your
drinking in certain places, with certain people, or
during certain occasions. When you see the pattern
to your drinking, you can think of ways to break the
pattern, break the chain of events that leads to
drinking. Think of ways you can alter or avoid situations that lead to drinking. The first part of Chapter 5 (Change of Scene) discusses some ways to remove
and avoid.

Remove. Put all your drinking related things in
one place out of the way. Don't have a wine decanter
on the table or a flask in your desk drawer. If you
plan to stop drinking, get all alcohol out of the
house. You might want to give your money to your
spouse or a friend so you can't buy alcohol.

Avoid. Until your drinking is under control,
avoid those situations where you usually drink or
there is most pressure on you to drink. Thus for a
while you might avoid bars, parties, dining out, certain friends, or stressful situations.

ALTERNATIVES

Look for alternatives to drinking. If you drink
alcohol to quench your thirst, drink something else
instead, such as juice or water. In drinking situations
drink something non-alcoholic such as tonic water and
lime without alcohol or bloody Mary mix without vodka.

139

Look for non-drinking activities to do when you feel
the urge to drink or when you wish to avoid the urge,
activities such as exercise or a hobby. Find new
social activities that do not require drinking, such
as sports, organized games, and movies.

How much do your friends influence your drinking?
Review the "Reactions of Others" on your written records. Are you locked into a group of friends in which
drinking is an important part of what you do? Perhaps
you should develop non-drinking activities with your
friends. Perhaps you should add some new friends. Perhaps you should avoid some of your old friends.

If there is a lot of social pressure on you to
drink, practice ways of refusing to drink. Here the
techniques of mental rehearsal (Chapter 12) will be
very useful. Practice what you will say in different
situations ("Not right now, thank you." "I've reached
my limit." "I'm the driver." "I'm taking medication.")
Practice what you will say under strong pressure.

DECREASING DESIRES
Observe and study your desire to drink. Be honest
with yourself! Review your records about your desires.
Then consult the last half of Chapter 10 (Out of Habit)
for ways to work with and decrease your desires.

CUTTING DOWN
Using our strategy of small steps, gradually start
cutting down on how much you drink. Here are a number
of ways to do it. You should do these and reward yourself for doing them.

Slow down your drinking. This is useful for almost everyone. Learn to sip your drink rather than
gulp it down. Set your drink down between sips and
space out your drinking. You might set a time limit
for yourself, such as only so many sips in 15 minutes
or so many drinks in an hour or an evening. If you
use time limits, it is good to decide on them in advance.

Gradually phase into drinks of lower alcoholic
content. To do this become more familiar with the al-
cohlic content of various drinks. If you usually drink
straight liquor, start by phasing into liquor plus
mix. Then switch to beer or wine.

Cut back on the situations in which you drink.

From your records of situations and desires (1-5) rank
order the situations in terms of how much you want or
need to drink in the situation. The top of the list
are situations where the desire is strongest (ratings
of 1) and the bottom of the list are situations with
the weakest desire (5). Then start at the bottom of
the list and eliminate drinking in that situation.
After you can do that, eliminate drinking in the situation second from the bottom. And so you gradually
move up through the whole list.

Now do the same with times of day. Divide the
day into blocks of time and rank order them from times
you drink the most (top of the list) to times you drink
the least. Then eliminate all drinking during the time
block on the bottom of the list. When you can do this,
move to the next time block and so on up the list.

Step by step you will gradually reduce your drinking until you are not drinking too much. Good for you!
Then continue reducing your drinking until you are not
drinking at all. Don't drink for a few months until
you have broken all aspects of the habit and all associations to drinking.

You can do it. Just take a step at a time.

STAYING FREE

Even after you have stopped drinking you should
continue those parts of your program that still apply,
such as learning better ways to handle your feelings,
reducing thoughts that have led to drinking, and
practicing resisting social pressure to drink.

Occasionally get out your long list of reasons
for not drinking too much and read through it and
think about it.

If you slip and start drinking again, don't panic.
Improve your program and work to stop again.

If your drinking problem was not too severe, then
after a few months you may choose to drink occasionally.
However, if this leads you back into problem drinking,
then controlled drinking may not be for you. No
drinking may be the best solution. If you are not
sure if you are drinking too much, keep written records of amount drunk for a couple of weeks.

But whichever way you go, you can get control of

your drinking rather than have it control you. You
will then improve your health, your mind, and your life.
This is something to be very proud of.

SUGGESTED READING

Miller, W. R. & Munoz, R. F. How to control your
    drinking. Prentice-Hall, 1976.

CHAPTER NINETEEN

SEX

People have many different attitudes, beliefs, and feelings about sex. People are influenced by the culture they are raised in and the attitudes and beliefs of their parents, friends, and religious teachers. People are also influenced by the type of sexual education they receive and their own sexual experiences. The purpose of this chapter is not to tell you what you should or should not do or what is moral. Rather, the purpose is to help you better accomplish what you consider desirable and right.

Sex between two people can be much more than an act of pleasure or a way to produce children. It can be an expression of love, a form of communication, an act of mutual giving and surrender, and a blending of individuals into something more than individual experience. But for most people there are many obstacles between them and the most fulfilling sex. This chapter shows you how to remove many of these obstacles.

UPTIGHTNESS

Most people are very uptight about sex. The American culture is very uptight about sex. For many people it is a topic they feel uncomfortable talking about; it is considered too personal. It is often emotionally tied up in a person's sense of manhood or womanhood. Thus it is usually easier for a person to say he or she is hooked on cigarettes than to admit to being sexually impotent. Yet both are common problems in daily living and it is usually easier to cure the impotence than the cigarette addiction.

Because people are so touchy and anxious about talking about sex, there is very poor communication about sex between sexual partners and between parents and their children. This results in many problems, including couples not getting the most from their sex life and children receiving poor sex education. It also carries over into general attitudes of the culture. There is something questionable about a culture that allows its children to watch very violent movies in which people are hurt and killed, yet forbids children to see many forms of expression of love which are considered to be too sexual.

143

INADEQUATE EDUCATION

Because Americans are so uptight about sex and because of various moral beliefs about sex, most Americans receive a very inadequate sexual education, whether in the home or elsewhere. This inadequate education is then a major cause of people feeling uptight and anxious about sex. So the inadequate education and uptightness continually support each other. It is thus necessary to break out of this trap.

Parents and friends do most of the sex education in America. But since most of them have had a limited sexual education, they can only pass on their own thoughts based on their own experiences, as well as their own fears, biases, and misunderstandings. In addition, most parents feel anxious talking about sex with their children so they don't communicate well, don't answer questions well, and/or don't sense what the child can best understand.

The schools are a second source of sex education; but many people have strong feelings about whether schools should be doing this and/or what should be covered. Many parents are concerned that if their children learn about it, they will do it. The schools have thus been very restricted and have usually limited themselves to discussing the biology of sex and/or attitudes about sex.

Other sources of sex education are not much better. Although there are some good sex manuals (see suggested readings), there are also some terrible ones and most are inadequate or poor. Information from friends may contain some true and useful things, but it usually also contains myths, rumors, exaggerations, and preposterous claims. The family doctor is often the resource for sexual problems. But he or she probably has not had any more formal sex education than you. Our culture is so uptight about sex we have not even educated our doctors adequately, a situation which is now slowly changing.

The point of all this is that most people have received a very poor sexual education and have learned many incorrect things. So if you have any type of sexual problem, be sure to get the facts. Don't assume that you know everything and don't assume that everything you know is correct. Get the facts!

TROUBLESOME BELIEFS

Here are some common examples of attitudes and misperceptions that impair people's sexual satisfaction. These troublesome beliefs, uncovered by researchers Masters and Johnson and others, result from inadequate education and social-religious influences.

Error 1. Women need not or should not experience pleasure. In the first half of this century in America a dominant point of view was that sex was something that women did to have children and/or something they put up with to satisfy their husbands' needs. Sex was at best necessary and at worst disgusting or painful. Few men devoted much attention to maximizing their partners' pleasure. Of course, there were many exceptions to these attitudes, and these beliefs are rapidly changing. But there are still many people who tend to think this way. The facts: Sex can be very pleasant to everyone involved if each person learns how to best please his or her partner.

Error 2. Women have one orgasm which produces satisfaction. Since this is generally true of men, men have fostered the belief it is also true for women. The facts: Some women are satisfied after one orgasm. Some women occasionally have several orgasms in a row. There are great individual differences among women.

Error 3. Women can have two different types of orgasm, clitoral and vaginal. Some women believe that one type is better than the other and/or it is important to experience both types. The facts: There is only one type of orgasm, although one's experience of it may vary from time to time.

Error 4. A man naturally knows what is pleasing to his partner. Although people may not think of it this way, this is a very widespread belief. Because of this belief most men would be too embarrassed to admit to their partners they don't know the best way to sexually please them. The facts: Most men have had an inadequate sexual education. Also there are tremendous differences among women; what is pleasing to one is not necessarily pleasing to another. Thus the wise man or woman learns to ask his or her partner about these things.

Error 5. The size of the penis is very important in satisfying a woman. Many men are very concerned about the size of their penises. The facts: Although

145

some women prefer penises of a certain size or shape,
most women are very pleased with their partner's penis
regardless of size. Also, although there are differences among the sizes of unerect penises, these differences are much less among erect penises. Finally, the
woman's vaginal muscles usually contract to fit whatever the size of the penis. Thus the size of an unerect penis is not that important in satisfying a
woman.

Error 6. The male above position in intercourse
is the best position and/or the only moral position.
The male above position is also called the missionary
position because Christian missionaries traveled
around the world teaching that all other positions
were sinful. A number of years ago most of the states
in America had laws against practicing any other position. The male above position is still the most popular and many people feel very uncomfortable with any
other position. The facts: Christ did not teach the
necessity of this position. In terms of maximizing
both partners' pleasure, other positions, such as the
female above position, may be preferable. Or it may
be best to use two or more positions during a love-
making session and/or over a period of time.

Error 7. Optimal sexual intercourse involves
both partners having orgasm at the same time. This
simultaneous orgasm is the stated goal of many sex
manuals. The facts: Optimal sex involves the pleasure
of both partners, regardless of whether or not there
is simultaneous orgasm. You may try to have simultaneous orgasm if you wish, but it should not be the goal
of intercourse. Better goals would be in terms of
love, pleasure, communication, and union.

Many other troublesome beliefs could be listed,
but this is not a book on sex education. Rather, from
these examples you can see the types of traps many
people fall into. It may be that some of the obstacles
in your way are based on similar beliefs or attitudes
that you have always accepted but never really thought
about. It is always useful to question why you believe something. Get the facts. See whether you have
an attitude that needs changing. Don't cling to your
approach to sex just because that is how you have always done it. Be flexible; try new things. Relax,
don't be uptight.

146

SEXUAL DEVELOPMENT

Most Americans become sexually mature before they have the opportunity to engage in sexual intercourse. Many people are sexually mature before they even begin dating. When this is coupled with inadequate sex education it can lead to many problems. Let us consider one possibility. Johnny is 13 years old and has little interest in dating yet. He enjoys wrestling around with the girl down the street, but that is all. However, Johnny is sexually mature physically and occasionally sexually aroused, although he doesn't know why. In need of a sexual outlet Johnny has learned to masturbate when aroused. But what does Johnny think about while masturbating? Because of his inadequate sex education he does not think about a loving relationship with a women expressed in sexual intercourse. Rather he might think about wrestling with the girl down the street. Now over time this leads him to associate sexual arousal with playing rough with women. When he is 18 he finds that he enjoys hurting women and is most aroused by fantasies of hurting women. In addition he finds he is not as sexually aroused by kissing or gentle caressing.

Now the above example is greatly oversimplified, but it illustrates some important points. People are often sexually mature and sexually arousable before they have associated sexual arousal with what might be considered the desirable or appropriate things. Left to their own and to chance they come to be sexually aroused and attracted by one or more of a wide range of things. This is particularly true of sexual fantasies during masturbation.

As a result people differ greatly in terms of what is sexually arousing. One person is attracted to thin women, another is attracted to fat women. One person is attracted to athletic looking men, another is attracted to studious looking men. One likes a dominant partner, another likes a submissive partner. Some people are most aroused when their partner is nude; others prefer their partners dressed in leather. People are aroused by a wide range of sexual fantasies.

What is sexually arousing to you depends on your experiences, the people you encountered, and the influences of your family and culture. Problems arise when your desires and needs can not be met, when your preferences limit your relationship with an important person, or when your desires or preferences lead you

147

to act in ways that hurt or offend others. In some of
these cases you may profit from professional help.

PROFESSIONAL HELP?
        Sexual problems can easily lead to more complex
personal and interpersonal problems. This is particularly true when the person is very sensitive and uptight
about sex and thus has difficulty talking about his or
her problem. As a result, sexual problems often lead
to more serious sexual dysfunctions, such as sexual
anxieties, lack of sexual responsiveness, inability to
achieve or maintain an erection, or inability to experience orgasm in intercourse. Sexual problems and
dysfunctions can then lead to interpersonal problems
and marriage difficulties, and these can lead to further problems.

        Therefore many people with sexual problems should
seek professional help in sorting out all the interrelated problems and doing something about them. This
is especially true if your problems are particularly
severe or complicated. See Chapter 28 (Choosing a
Counselor) for suggestions on finding the right professional to help.

        On the other hand, there are many things you can
do for yourself without professional help, as will be
described in the rest of this chapter. You will find
ways to overcome some common sexual problems. You will
also learn ways to improve your sex life even if you
have no major problems.

        In the remainder of this chapter,the first three
secions (1. Get the facts. 2. Know yourself. 3. Communication) apply to almost everyone who wishes to improve his or her sex life. The next three sections
(4. Medical checkup. 5. Anxiety. 6. General principles) apply to anyone with any type of sexual problem
or dysfunction. The last two sections (7. Specific
dysfunctions. 8. Sexual fantasies) deal with working
with some specific problem areas.

1.   GET THE FACTS
        Earlier in this chapter was discussed the inade-
quate sex education most people receive and some examples of common troublesome beliefs were given. The
point is that many sex problems are based on faulty
information, misperceptions, and irrational beliefs.
So the first thing to do is be sure you have your facts
right. If you believe a form of birth control will

decrease your sexual feelings, get the facts. If you
assume your partner enjoys a particular form of foreplay, ask your partner about it. If you are avoiding
professional treatment of your sexual dysfunction because of what you think may be involved, talk to some
possible therapists.

Getting the facts may involve reading some books
about sex and/or counsulting a psychologist, sex therapist, or marriage counselor. Getting the facts should
always involve discussions with your partner, as
described below. Getting the facts also includes
better understanding your own attitudes and beliefs
about sex.

2. KNOW YOURSELF
As discussed throughout this whole book, it is
always useful and important to get to know yourself
better. This is particularly true in the area of sex
where people's uptightness keeps them from knowing
themselves very well.

Make friends with your body. Don't be uptight
about your body. Relax. Many people can't undress in
front of their partners. Many people feel uncomfortable if their partners look at their bodies. Many
people have to make love in the dark because they are
too self-conscious about their bodies. Relax and make
friends with your body.

Know your body. Many women have never looked
closely at their genitals. Many men consider it per-
verted to look very closely at their penises. Most
people have never looked very carefully at their bodies.
Make friends with your body and get to know it better.
Stand nude in front of a mirror and look at your body
in detail. Don't judge your body; just get to know
it better. Take small steps! Don't push yourself or
get too anxious. Take your time and gradually get to
know and love your body more and more. Chapter 6
(Relaxing Body and Mind) and Chapter 13 (Nutrition
and Exercise) include suggestions on getting to know
your body better.

Next get to know your partner's body better and
let him or her know your body better. Take small steps!
Don't progress too fast for either yourself or your
partner. Rather, gradually let each other see and
touch the other's body and get to know it better.

Know your thoughts. What are your thoughts about
sex when approached, during foreplay, during intercourse, afterwards, and other times? It might be useful to keep a written log of your thoughts. After de-
termining what you think about sex, it is important to
evaluate these thoughts. Are some of your thoughts
based on faulty beliefs or lack of information? If so,
get the facts. Are some of your thoughts irrational,
self-defeating, or anxiety-producing? If so, you may
wish to change some of these with the procedures of
Chapter 11 (What Do You Think). Do you have specific
attitudes and preferences about sexual behavior? If
so, then you should discuss these with your partner.

Know your feelings. Know the emotions you feel
in different sexual situations. Are there some feelings, such as anxiety, that need to be reduced? Know
your likes and dislikes and communicate these to your
partner.

3. COMMUNICATION

Communicating with your partner about your sexual
preferences and problems is the most important thing
you can do to generally enhance your sex life and/or
overcome specific sexual problems. You and your partner can improve your sexual interactions by better communicating to each other your particular likes and dislikes. For example, you may find there are some sexual
fantasies that the two of you can play with.

Similarly, if you have a sexual problem and a regular sexual partner, you can best work on the problem if
your partner understands about the problem and can help
you. The two of you working together is the best approach. When two people are involved in a relationship, a sexual problem is not the problem of one person.
Both people are involved and should work together.

Unfortunately, because people are so uptight about
sex, they often find talking about sex to be uncomfortable. Thus many people are poor communicators when
it comes to sex, when this is a topic that needs much
better communication. So work at communicating more
with your partner about sexual things. Don't push
yourself too fast. Take small steps and gradually communicate more and more. Open up at your own rate; but
keep moving toward greater communication. Similarly,
encourage more communication from your partner, but
don't push him or her too fast. Take small steps. Respect your partner's feelings and preferences; don't

judge or evaluate them. Emphasize how you can improve things; don't spend time on who is at fault. Try to come up with specific, positive ideas and plans. See Chapter 27 (Communication) for more on improving communication.

Have open discussions with your partner about sexual topics of importance to one or both of you. If these discussions do not naturally occur often enough, then set aside or schedule specific times for such discussions. It is _very_ important that you create enough time for these discussions! The following are some possible topics for discussion: how each person initiates and declines sexual activity and how this makes the other person feel, preferences and opinions about various foreplay activities and intercourse positions, ways to make sex more pleasurable and/or more varied, attitudes and preferences about various sexual practices such as masturbation and oral-genital activities, frequency and location of having sex, and the possible use of erotic material such as books and magazines.

Many people's sex life eventually becomes fairly stereotyped and routine. Intercourse is basically practiced in the same way in the same places at the same times. There are no more surprises or improvisations. Look for ways of adding more variety to your sex life. Communicate with your partner about what could be done here.

"Sensate focus" is a very useful practice for sexual partners to communicate and learn about improving their sexual activities. It is a practice in touching each other and communicating preferences. To begin each session of sensate focus set aside a time and place in which you won't be disturbed. Next, create a relaxing and pleasing setting. This might involve soft music in the background, incense, and/or glasses of wine. Lights need to be on, but can be dim.

Begin by lying nude together and just talking.(If this is too upsetting, begin with some clothes on and then gradually remove the clothes. Take your time, even if it involves doing it gradually during several sessions over a few days. Take small steps.) Spend some time just lying near each other and talking. Talk about pleasant things, not topics of conflict or anxiety.

The next step involves touching each other. This

151

step can be begun on the first session of sensate focus or you may prefer to wait until a later session. Here you take turns giving and receiving. First one person is the receiver and is touched and caressed by the other, the giver. Then after a while you switch who is giver and receiver. When you are the giver you gently touch, stroke, caress, and kiss the other person, avoiding breasts and genitals. When you are the receiver you tell the giver what you like most about what he or she is doing. Emphasize what you like, not what you don't like. Give positive and specific suggestions to the giver about how to do something so it is most pleasurable to you. This may be done verbally, as in verbal suggestions or reactions, and/or non-verbally, as in guiding the giver's hand.

When you are the giver you should be learning how to better please your partner. Don't be upset because you learn things you did not know. Don't be upset because what you learn surprises you or leads you to change the way you please your partner. Don't be upset. Relax. Make it easy for the receiver to tell you things.

After one person has been the receiver for a while, say 10 to 20 minutes, switch roles so the other person is the receiver. Switch back and forth until you feel that is enough for one day's session.

For the next session of sensate focus continue doing what you were doing before, but now add in touching and caressing the breasts and genitals. Move slowly here if you feel uncomfortable. Again take turns being giver and receiver. Do not stimulate the other person to orgasm. Do not treat this as foreplay to intercourse. Avoid intercourse at this time and just communicate about what is most pleasurable. Do this practice for two or more sessions and then do it every now and then for the next few years. Later variations of sensate focus can involve rubbing lotions into each other's skin, practicing massage, and bathing or showering together.

Some time spent doing sensate focus with your partner will probably improve your sex life, facilitate communication, and perhaps reduce some sexual anxiety.

4. MEDICAL CHECKUP
    Many sexual dysfunctions are caused by physical problems. For example, for some women painful inter-

course or inability to have an orgasm may have a physical cause. Similarly for some impotent men the cause is physical. In most cases the physical problem can be treated quite easily. So if you have a sexual dysfunction of any type, the best first step is to get a physical checkup by a doctor familiar with physical causes of sexual disorders. Remember that only a few doctors have such training; so ask them first or get a referral.

5. ANXIETY

Anxiety is the major cause of most sexual problems and dysfunctions. Anxiety in a male may cause inadequate arousal, inability to achieve or maintain an erection, tendency to ejaculate too quickly, or inability to ejaculate during intercourse. Anxiety in a female may cause inadequate arousal, too little lubrication for intercourse, excessive tension in the vaginal muscles, or inability to have an orgasm.

The possible causes of the anxiety are many. First is the general uptightness most people feel toward sex or some aspects of sex. Added to this for some people is the anxiety that results from some previous, perhaps unpleasant, sexual experiences. Then for some people there is anxiety about their sexual performance. For example, a man is impotent one time and is now anxious he will be impotent again. But the anxiety he feels makes it more likely he will be impotent again. So pretty soon the man is impotent most of the time, all because of anxiety.

The way out of all this, of course, is to relax. When you are involved in sex do not be concerned about how well you will perform. Forget about such goals. Just relax and enjoy the pleasure of the here and now. Chapter 6 (Relaxing Body and Mind) suggests ways to help you relax more. If your anxiety is based on a particular fear or unpleasant past experience, then review Chapter 15 (Fears). Relax. The following general principles can further help you relax and be less goal-oriented.

6. GENERAL PRINCIPLES

Here are some general principles which are useful in overcoming many sexual problems and dysfunctions.

First it is important to have realistic expectations. Some people have ideas about what "perfect" sexual intercourse should be like and then are disap-

153

pointed when it doesn't turn out the way they think it should. Now if these ideas are unrealistic, the people are not enjoying sex as much as they could. Reality is that sometimes you have an orgasm and sometimes you don't. Sometimes you hold ejaculation for a long time and sometimes you don't. Sometimes you have simultaneous orgasm and sometimes you don't. It is good to want to improve your sex life. But don't set unrealistic goals. And don't be upset when things don't go the way you want or expect. Rather, try to always enjoy sex, regardless of the outcome.

Take small steps. Go slowly and stay relaxed. If you have problems during intercourse, approach intercourse very gradually. Build up your sexual arousal and response in a non-intercourse situation, such as a variation of sensate focus. Then gradually over days slowly move more and more in the direction of intercourse. Take your time! Stay relaxed. Review the use of hierarchies described in Chapter 15 (Fears) and apply the same approach here.

During sex forget about goals. Having some goal in mind impairs your sex and is bad for sexual problems. Remember the example of the man who was anxious he might be impotent and then the anxiety made him impotent. Forget about goals. Intercourse is often not the best immediate goal. And orgasm is not the sole measure of successful sex. Forget about goals and immerse yourself in the pleasure of the sexual activities you are involved in at the present.

Vary your sex life. One way to help break out of old problems is the strategy of Change of Scene (Chapter 5). Your sexual problems have become associated with where and how you have sex. Thus by changing these you break some of the associations and weaken the problems. So when you are ready to change some of your sexual behaviors, look for ways to change the time and place you have sex and the way you approach it. Look for ways to change the setting, such as by rearranging furniture of altering the lighting.

These principles apply to almost all sexual problems. Next are strategies for specific problems, strategies built on these principles.

7. SPECIFIC DYSFUNCTIONS
     In this section are some ways of working with common specific sex problems. For many people these sug-

gestions will be enough. However, if this is not enough
for you or if you have trouble accomplishing what you
want, be sure to seek some professional assistance
(see Chapter 28, Choosing a Counselor).

Too little arousal. A person may find that she or
he is often not as sexually aroused as desired. Sexual
activities may not lead to the amount of sexual arousal
necessary to enjoy sex most. Too little arousal may
keep a person from having an orgasm. There are several
things that can be done here.

First you should determine whether any feelings
of anxiety may be part of the problem. This is very
common. If so, then you should work on reducing the
anxiety as discussed earlier in this chapter and
elsewhere in the book (Chapters 6, 7, 11, 15). Next
you should better communicate to your partner, as discussed earlier, those things which are sexually arousing to you. This includes places and times you make
love, ways you like to be approached and touched, and
ways you enjoy making love. It might also involve incense, perfume, pornography, or vibrators. If you are
not sure yourself about what is most pleasurable, then
you and your partner should experiment with different
things and different ways. Finally, sexual fantasies
often affect sexual arousal. This will be discussed
later in this chapter.

Non-orgasmic female. Some women seldom or never
have an orgasm. If you aren't sure whether you have
ever had an orgasm, you probably haven't. Often the
cause is physical and can usually be easily corrected.
Sometimes the doctor or sex counselor can recommend
some exercises to strengthen vaginal muscles, particularly Kegel exercises for the pubococcygeus muscles
Strengthening these muscles can make intercourse more
pleasurable for both parnters and give the woman more
control over unintentional urinating. Often the woman
is non-orgasmic because the male partner does not
sexually interact with her in the best way. In this
case the male needs to learn how to better please the
woman and help her have an orgasm. This may involve
trying different positions, better communication and/
or professional guidance.

Another major cause is anxiety: anxiety due to
previous experiences, anxiety about having an orgasm
or "losing control," or some other form of anxiety.
When this is the case, the anxiety must be dealt with,

155

as discussed earlier. Another major cause is too little arousal, which should be treated as outlined in the previous section.

After you have dealt with all the above, then continue as follows: Be sure your partner understands your problem and is willing to help. Everything at this time should be aimed toward your pleasure and arousal. Then _slowly_ move in the direction of intercourse. Take small steps. Continue foreplay until you feel very aroused. If this doesn't happen, do not continue on to intercourse! Rather, stop for the day, relax, and appreciate the pleasure you had. Then return another day and start again. Take small steps! When you reach the time of being very aroused during foreplay, then slowly move into intercourse. You, not your male partner, should set the pace. You may find it best to use a female above position at this point. Next gradually insert the penis, relax, withdraw the penis, and relax. Continue to do this a couple of times. If your arousal decreases a lot, stop for the day and begin with foreplay again another time.

When you can stay aroused with the penis inside you, gradually introduce rhythmic movement. Again, you should set the pace and rhythm. Continue to do this in a way which is most pleasing to you. Do not try to have an orgasm; just relax and enjoy yourself. Do not think about having an orgasm; just lose yourself in your feelings of the moment. If you continue this practice over a number of days, you will probably begin to have orgasms. Relax and take small steps.

Be sure to tell your partner how much you appreciate his concern and help. Tell him in detail those things which were the most useful and pleasurable to you. Then gradually move toward a form of sexual relationship and intercourse that satisfies both of your interests and needs.

Impotent male. Impotence refers to when a man can not achieve an erection or can not maintain it long enough for successful intercourse. This periodically happens to most men. So if it happens every once in a while, don't be concerned. But if it happens quite often, then you may want to do something about it.

Anxiety and/or fear of failure are the most common causes of impotence. If this is part of your problem, you need to deal with the anxiety as discussed

earlier in this chapter and elsewhere in this book
(Chapters 6, 7, 11, 15). Drinking too much alcohol is
another common cause. If this is part of your problem,
see the previous chapter on how to reduce your drinking.
Also remember there are many physical causes of impotence. So if anxiety and alcohol are not the causes,
you should consult a doctor familiar with possible physical problems.

After you have done the above, then the rest of
your program should follow these steps: Tell your
partner about your problem and get her help. Next
set aside some times you can work on the problem, times
when you can be relaxed and not rushed. Then lie together and engage in the types of sexual activities, other
than intercourse, that you most enjoy. Relax and take
your time. Next gradually be stimulated to an erection.
This can be done by your partner and/or you, with hands
or mouth, or whatever is best for you. When an erection
occurs, do not attempt intercourse! Rather, stop stimulating the penis and let the erection decrease. Then
after a few minutes of relaxing, stimulate it to an
erection again, and then let it decrease again. Do
this a number of times and then stop for the day. Do
not attempt intercourse. Do this stimulation practice
for a few days. Continue this practice until you can
easily maintain an erection outside of intercourse.

When you have mastered the above, you slowly start
moving toward intercourse. Relax and take small steps.
Begin by you and/or your partner stimulating your penis
to erection. Then gradually insert the penis in your
partner, perhaps using the female above position. After
you have inserted somewhat, withdraw,and relax. Wait a
few minutes, stimulate the penis, insert again, and
withdraw again. Each time stay inside your partner a
little longer. But don't begin any other movement or
seek orgasm. Simply lie quietly together with your
penis inside. Continue this practice over several or
many days until you can maintain an erection inside
your partner for a moderate amount of time.

When you can do the above, then gradually introduce sexual movement while inside. Relax and take your
time. Slowly continue until you and your partner are
enjoying full sexual intercourse.

Maintaining an erection is a skill you can learn.
But you must relax and take small steps in your treatment.

Premature ejaculation. A common problem for many men is premature ejaculation, the tendency to ejaculate more quickly than desired. In some cases this may involve ejaculating before entering the female or soon after. In other cases the ejaculation occurs somewhat later, but still too soon to be most satisfying to the female. If it occurs once in a while, this is normal and not to be worried about. If it occurs more often, or more often than you want, then you can do something about it. Learning to control your ejaculation is a skill you can learn.

The first step, as in all sexual problems, is to determine whether you have any anxiety in sexual situations that could lead to premature ejaculation. Do you experience any anxiety or uptightness related to sexual intercourse? Are you anxious about how well you will perform? Are you anxious about having premature ejaculation? If you have any such anxiety, you need to deal with it first, as discussed earlier in this chapter and elsewhere in this book (Chapters 6, 7, 11, 15).

After reducing any anxiety, the next step is to gradually approach intercourse while keeping from ejaculating. You know when you feel ejaculation is nearing. The training consists of building up to this point and stopping before you need to ejaculate. You do this while taking small steps toward intercourse.

Begin with a partner who understands your problem and wants to help. Start just lying together during foreplay. Do what you would ordinarily find pleasurable, but slow everything down. Gradually move toward more and more stimulation of the penis, in whatever way you enjoy. But at this time avoid penis contact with the female sex organs. At any time you feel you are nearing the point where you may need to ejaculate, then stop what you are doing, relax, and let your sexual arousal decrease. After your arousal has died down and your penis has lost some or much of its erection, then begin sexual fondling again, including stimulation of the penis. Again, be sure to stop and relax just before you reach the need to ejaculate. Do this stimulate-and-relax a number of times, gradually increasing the amount of stimulating before the need to relax.

Continue the above practice for a number of days. Avoid intercourse during this time. Continue the practice until you can be stimulated for long periods without ejaculating. Take your time. Take small steps.

158

When you can withhold ejaculating quite well in this practice, then gradually move toward intercourse.

Begin by stimulating your penis to erection and then gradually introducing the penis into your partner. Again, if at any time you feel you are nearing the need to ejaculate, then withdraw, stop what you are doing, and relax! Then begin again. Gradually insert your penis. Just hold it inside without movement. Always withdraw and relax before you need to ejaculate. After you can withhold ejaculating when inside and not moving, then gradually introduce movement. Stop, withdraw, and relax before you ejaculate.

If you follow this practice, relax, and take small steps, you can gradually build up your ability to delay ejaculating. After you have developed this skill, you can use it to help you and your partner have the most rewarding sex life.

8. SEXUAL FANTASIES

Most people have some sexual fantasies, images or ideas which, when imagined or thought about, bring sexual pleasure and arousal. Imagining making love with someone is one of the most common sexual fantasies. The types of sexual fantasies vary greatly among people. One person fantasizes about making love to a movie star; another thinks about being seduced by a sales-person. One woman becomes sexually aroused if she imagines being forced into sex with a construction worker, although she would not want to be forced in real life. Another woman fantasizes about seducing teenage boys, but will never tell anybody about this. One man becomes sexually aroused when imagining being tied up and whipped by a woman; while another man fantasizes about spanking women. Some people fantasize sexual activities with people dressed in particular clothes, such as high heeled shoes, leather jackets or suits, or a uniform of some type. Other people fantasize about having sex in unusual places. The list of sexual fantasies could be continued on and on. Almost anything you can imagine is a sexual fantasy for someone.

A sexual fantasy is not necessarily good or bad in itself. It is what it leads you to think or do that is important. If the fantasy is simply a private dream that you use to improve your sex life, then it can be desirable and useful. On the other hand, the fantasy can lead you to think and act in ways which are un-

159

desirable. Examples here would be if the fantasy dom-
inates too much of your thinking, limits your perceptions or interactions with others, makes it more probable you will be aggressive or hurt someone, or leads
to some other behavior that is socially unacceptable or
illegal. This section considers sexual fantasies: how
to use them, change them, and reduce them.

In some cases the sexual fantasy merely reflects
sexual preferences that perhaps can be achieved in real
life. A man may have a sexual fantasy about women who
wear a particular type of nightgown. In this case the
man may be able to share his fantasy with a sexual
partner who will enjoy wearing such a nightgown. Discussion of sexual fantasies with your partner may lead
you both to find other ways of pleasing each other and/
or add variety to your sex life.

Fantasies and intercourse. Most people use sexual
fantasies before and during intercourse as a way to increase sexual arousal. This can often be helpful, particularly for people with some sexual problems, such as
non-orgasmic females. However, if a person must always
use a fantasy during intercourse, then he or she is
not fully experiencing and enjoying intercourse. Here
the fantasy is limiting. If this is true for you, then
this section tells you what to do.

Use your fantasy during intercourse up to the
point when you know orgasm is about to occur. Then
switch out of your fantasy and totally immerse yourself in the here and now of intercourse with your
partner as you have orgasm. Totally immerse yourself
in the feelings, sights, smells, and everything else
of this beautiful time. For many times continue this
practice of using your fantasy up till orgasm and then
letting the fantasy go at the last minute.

After you have done this a number of times, gradually start letting go of the fantasy earlier and earlier. The first step is to use the fantasy until almost to orgasm, then slide out of the fantasy into the
experiences of intercourse. The next step is to use
the fantasy again, but discontinue it a little earlier.
Gradually you let go of the fantasy earlier and earlier,
until eventually you do not need the fantasy at all.
You will have transferred some of the sexual arousal
from the fantasy to intercourse without the fantasy.
However, if any time during this practice you find you
are losing sexual arousal, then you can always drop

back into your fantasy for a few minutes.

It is very important when doing this that you take very small steps. It is better to move too slowly than too fast. You want to phase out your fantasy very gradually. This may take many months or more. But if you stay with it and are patient, eventually intercourse without the fantasy will be more arousing, pleasurable, and fulfilling than intercourse with the fantasy.

Another thing you can do to help all of this is to gradually incorporate your partner into your fantasy. If you are imagining making love to a movie star, then in your fantasy periodically replace the movie star with an image of your partner. Then switch back to the movie star. Taking small steps, gradually increase the amount of time your partner is in your fantasy. However, do not do this if your fantasy involves doing anything you would not want to do with your partner. For example, if your fantasy involves hurting someone, do not fantasize hurting your partner!

Fantasies and masturbation. Like everything else in the area of sex, there are many different points of view about masturbation. For some it is something that should never be done, perhaps because it is a religious sin or because it is too ego-centered. For others it is something only to be practiced when no appropriate sexual partner is available. For others it is a desirable sexual practice used in addition to intercourse. And for others it is felt to be preferable to intercourse. Numerous false myths have been told about how masturbation may lead to such things as insanity, hair on the hands, or going blind. No opinion on masturbation is being advocated here. But if you do masturbate with sexual fantasies, this is a time to build up sexual arousal to your sexual partner, possible partners, or intercourse in general.

The general strategy here is the same as above in the intercourse situation. Use your fantasy during masturbation until you feel you are about to have an orgasm. At that point switch into imagining intercourse with your partner or potential partner, as you continue into orgasm. Imagine intercourse with your partner as realistically as possible, living the scene rather than just picturing yourself in the scene. Imagine what you would feel and see. Continue this practice for many masturbation times.

Next gradually increase the amount of time during masturbation that you imagine intercourse with a realistic partner. Take small steps as you gradually increase here. Go back and forth between your sexual fantasy and imagining realistic intercourse. Continue this until you no longer need your sexual fantasy. That is, continue this practice until imagining intercourse with a realistic partner is arousing enough for masturbation to orgasm. Then stop using your previous sexual fantasy.

Reducing fantasies. There are two reasons why you might wish to reduce or eliminate a sexual fantasy: 1) you no longer need it, and/or 2) the fantasy is undesirable or harmful in some way.

If you have used your sexual fantasy, as described above, to increase sexual arousal in intercourse, then eventually you will no longer need your sexual fantasy. At this point you can just forget about it or occasionally use it. However, at this point you may also wish to focus all your sexual energy into intercourse and away from fantasies. You may consider your fantasy inappropriate or undesirable in some way and wish to be done with it. You may have always been ashamed or self-conscious of your fantasy.

Similarly, your fantasy may be undesirable for reasons such as those discussed earlier. That is, the fantasy may cause you to think, feel, or act in ways that are undesirable. Thus you help yourself by eliminating such a fantasy.

There are two steps to reducing or eliminating a sexual fantasy. First you should deal with the desires associated with the fantasy. Chapter 10 (Out of Habit) describes how to work with desires. Particularly useful in this chapter is the technique of "unpleasant associations." This involves associating, in your imagination, your sexual fantasy with something unpleasant. For example, a person with a sexual fantasy about being tied up might practice imagining scenes such as the following: The person imagines his usual fantasy about being tied up and then gradually makes the scene unpleasant by imagining becoming very sick and vomiting all over himself and the other person. Practice with such scenes reduces the sexual associations of the fantasy.

The second step in reducing or eliminating fantasies involves learning better control of your thoughts.

162

As described in Chapter 11 (What Do You Think) this
would include stopping the sexual fantasy when it occurs and replacing it with more desirable thoughts or
fantasies. Using these procedures you can eliminate
any fantasy you wish.

CONCLUSION
        Using the material in this chapter many people can
overcome sexual problems and/or generally improve their
sex lives. Three critical parts of this are improved
communication with your partner, relaxing and reducing
anxiety, and taking small steps.

        On the other hand, many sex problems have a phys-
ical base and require medical attention. And many
people would do best to consult a counselor for help
in these areas, rather than relying on what they can
do for themselves (see Chapter 28, Choosing a Counselor).

                    SUGGESTED READING

HUMAN SEXUALITY
        These are basic books about human sexuality, in-
cluding physical basis of sex, sexual behavior, common
myths, and social issues.
    Cohen, F. Understanding human sexuality. Prentice-
        Hall, 1974.
    Katchadowian, H. Human sexuality: sense and nonsense.
        W. H. Freeman, 1974.
    McCary, J. L. Sexual myths and fallacies. Van
        Nostrand, 1971.

OVERCOMING SEXUAL PROBLEMS
        Belliveau and Richter provide an introductory over-
view of the findings of Masters and Johnson regarding
the human sexual response and treatment of sexual dysfunctions. Brown and Fauldner discuss ways to increase
intimacy, improve physical understanding of each other,
and overcome many specific dysfunctions. Heiman and
the LoPiccolos describe a program for non-orgasmic
women to be able to have orgasms. Kass and Stauss
provide step by step instructions for some sexual activities including stroking, massage, masturbation,
and intercourse. Nowinski discusses issues of male
sexual expectations and behavior, including anxiety,
erection problems, delaying or accelerating orgasm,
communication, body-awareness, and particularly attitudes and roles. Zeiss and Zeiss provide a complete

program for overcoming premature ejaculation.

Belliveau, F. & Richter, L. Understanding human
    sexual inadequacy. Little Brown, 1970; Bantam
    paperback, 1970
Brown, P. & Fauldner, C. Treat yourself to sex: a
    guide to good loving. Penguin Books, 1977.
Heiman, J., LoPiccolo, L. & LoPiccolo, J. Becoming
    orgasmic: a program of sexual growth for women.
    Prentice-Hall, 1976.
Kass, D. J. & Stauss, F. F. Sex therapy at home.
    Simon & Schuster, 1975.
Nowinski, J. Becoming satisfied: a man's guide
    to sexual fulfillment. Prentice-Hall, 1980.
Zeiss, R. A. & Zeiss, A. Prolong your pleasure.
    Pocket Books paperback, 1978.

IMPROVING SEX
    Masters and Johnson discuss a number of topics of
sexual behavior within a marriage. Topics include
sexual pleasure, double standards, extramarital sex,
sexual fidelity, touching, and commitment. Ellis
emphasizes a positive attitude toward sex. Downing
provides one of many comprehensive books on massage.
Comfort's book is useful as a source of stimulation,
things to try,and topics to discuss on the way to exploring and enhancing your own sexual interests,
attitudes and behaviors.

Masters, W. H. & Johnson, V.E. The pleasure bond.
    Little Brown, 1975. Bantam paperback, 1976.
Ellis. A. Sex without guilt. Lancer Books, 1966.
Downing, G. The massage book. Random House, 1972.
Comfort, A. The joy of sex. Crown Publishing, Inc.,
    1972; Fireside (Simon & Schuster) paperback.

CHAPTER TWENTY

LEARNING AND REMEMBERING

How well you learn and remember something depends on many things, including how interesting and important what you are learning is, how what you are learning relates to other things you know, and how often you will put into use what you learn. But the most important effect on your memory is how well you originally learn what you want to remember. The better you learn it, the better you will remember it. This chapter will give you some suggestions on how to learn better and thus remember better.

MEMORY AIDS

In addition to the suggestions for learning in this chapter, you should also review the discussion of memory aids in Chapter 9 (Getting Organized). Part of improving learning and remembering is developing various memory aids, such as lists and a daily calendar, that help you remember. These free your mind for other tasks, including other things to learn and remember.

ATTENTION

The first step to better learning and remembering is to pay better attention to what it is you wish to learn. This may sound obvious, but it is a common problem. If when you are learning something, your attention is drifting and your mind is wandering, you won't learn it well. People who have trouble remembering the names of others they just met often don't pay enough attention to the names when introduced.

It is important to practice paying better attention. Keep your attention focused on what you are learning. Try to keep your attention and mind from being distracted or pulled in other directions. Keeping a focused attention is a skill that will improve with practice. So practice paying better attention. Learning to keep focused attention is helped by the meditation practice described in Chapter 6 (Relaxing Body and Mind).

When paying attention to what you are learning, look for any special features that might help you remember. For example, when learning a person's name, look carefully at him or her and notice any specific

165

characteristics that catch your eye, such as the person having large blue eyes or being quite tall. Look carefully for a few distinctive characteristics. Then try to associate the name with the characteristics. If a tall person is named Wayne, you might associate his being tall with the tall actor John Wayne, and thus remember the name Wayne. Another approach to remembering names involves imagining the person dressed in some way that you associate with his name. If a person has a name such as Roman, try to see the person as an ancient Roman complete with Roman toga. How would you remember the name of a person named Baker or Marshall? It might involve seeing Baker as a baker complete with chef's hat and apron or seeing Marshall as a western marshall with gun and badge.

As another example of looking for special characteristics, consider wanting to learn the phone number 468-1357. What might you notice? One possibility is that you would see that the first three digits are three even numbers in order, while the last four digits are the first four odd numbers in order. Noticing this might help you better learn and remember this phone number.

ASSOCIATION

Most learning involves associating things together, such as associating a person's name with his face. So you more easily learn something if you can associate it with something you already know and/or something you can remember easily. Many things can be better remembered if you associate them with verbal phrases, rhymes, and mental images.

For example, when you are standing on a boat facing the bow, the right side is called "starboard" and the left side is called "port." How can you remember this? One way is to remember the phrase that you just left port on the boat. This associates "port" with left. To remember that in setting a table the fork goes on the left side of the plate, you might think of the mechanical device called a forklift. How do you spell the word for the head of a school: "principle" or "principal?" The second is correct and can be remembered by thinking of the principal as being a pal. When going on and off daylight savings time, you can remember which way to change your clocks with the phrase "Spring forward and Fall back." In the Spring move your clock forward one hour; in the Fall move it back one hour.

Rhymes are often useful as in the rhyme "Thirty days has September..." which helps you remember the number of days in a month. A common rhyme to help in spelling is "i before e except after c." This can be made more accurate as "i before e except after c or when it sounds like a as in neighbor or weigh."

Some associations are based on using the first letters of words. To remember the notes on the lines of a music staff you can remember the phrase "every good boy does fine." The first letters of this phrase (EGBDF) are the notes in order. The notes in between the lines spell FACE. The first letters of the Great Lakes spell HOMES, which can then help you remember the lakes. Do you know them? The colors of the visual spectrum, in order, are red, orange, yellow, green, blue indigo, and violet. To help you remember this you can remember that the first letters of the colors spell the name ROY G. BIV.

In caves, various formations, often columns and cones, build from the floor and ceiling. Those that come down from the ceiling are called "stalactites," and those that go up from the floor are called "stalagmites." How can you remember which is which? One way focuses on the letter c versus the letter g: stalactites are from the ceiling and stalagmites are from the ground. Another way focuses on the visual imagery of T vs M: stalactite has the T which looks like something hanging from the ceiling, while the M of stalagmite looks like something building up from the ground. My favorite way is based on the difference between mite and tite in the two words. Just remember the expression "ants in the pants." This reminds you that when the mites go up, the tights go down.

One way of remembering numbers is to change the numbers into corresponding letters or words that may be easier to remember. Many phone numbers can be replaced by words using letters that correspond to the numbers on the phone dial. For example, the number 382-5467 can be translated into DUCK HOP which may be easier to remember. Later you can just dial DUCK HOP on the phone. In mathematics there is the constant pi, the ratio of the circumference of a circle to its diameter. The value of pi is an unending decimal that begins 3.14159265358979.... One way to remember this is with the phrase "How I want a drink, alcoholic of course, after the heavy chapters involving quantum mechanics." The number of letters of each word in the phrase gives you the sequence of digits of pi.

MENTAL IMAGERY

Generally the most effective memory technique is to associate what you wish to remember with a mental image or picture. Many people remember the shape of Italy by thinking it is shaped like a boot. Above it was mentioned how you could remember a person's name is Marshall by picturing him as a western marshall.

When using mental imagery, the more unusual or silly the image, the better. It will be easier to remember the name Marshall if the image of a western marshall that you use is very unusual, dramatic, or funny. Similarly, remember the use of the word HOMES to help remember the names of the Great Lakes? Now how do you remmeber the word HOMES? One way would be to use mental imagery and imagine an unusual and spectacular scene of homes sinking into the Great Lakes.

Or consider the example where we translated a person's phone number (382-5467) into the words DUCK HOP. Now we need to associate these words with the person. We would use some mental image such as seeing the person hopping with a duck or doing a dance called the "duck hop." The stranger or funnier the image, the better.

You are at a party and want to practice remembering names. The first person you meet is Jan. You are careful to pay attention when you hear her name. You also pay attention to her face and appearance, noticing any distinguishing characteristics. You notice she has long blond hair. Now you associate the name with her appearance, focusing on her hair. Here is the place for mental imagery. For example, you might change the name Jan into the word "jam" and construct an image of the person with her hair filled with jam. Later when you see her, her hair will again catch your attention and trigger your mental image of jam in the hair. This image will lead you to think of jam which will remind you of the name Jan.

All of this might sound quite involved; but it is pretty easy after you have been doing it for a little while. With some practice you can use mental imagery in many situations to help you remember. If you want to remember you left your glasses on the television, you can develop a mental image of the television with the antenna going through the lenses of the glasses.

Consider the following situation: You are driving in your car when you suddenly remember that it is very important that you mail a letter when you get home in a few hours. How would you use mental imagery to help you remember to mail the letter? You want to develop a mental image that will associate the letter with something you will see as soon as you get home. For example, you might practice imagining seeing the letter tied with ribbons to the front door handle. Later when you see the door handle, it reminds you of the letter.

MEMORY SYSTEMS

There are many complex memory systems based on the principles discussed above. These systems are called mnemonic systems.

One system is based on the following code of numbers and words: one is bun, two is shoe, three is tree, four is door, five is hive, six is sticks, seven is heaven, eight is gate, nine is line, and ten is hen. Now if you want to remember that Bob's address is 8710, you convert the numbers into the words gate, heaven, and hen. Then you develop a funny mental image, such as of Bob opening the gate of heaven and seeing a bunch of hens run out.

There are many such memory systems, some of them quite complex. All these systems take a while to learn to use. But then they can be used to remember more than previously could have been remembered. Memory-expert entertainers use these types of memory systems. However, such systems are not necessary for most people who can get along with the principles discussed in this chapter. If you wish to learn more about memory systems, see the suggested readings at the end of this chapter.

STUDYING

The rest of this chapter deals with studying, as for students taking courses. Studying is an important skill for people in school. But the schools seldom teach people how to study; students are just told to go and do it. As a result most high school and college students do not know how to study well.

Good studying is a skill to be acquired. Hence it takes some work and time to learn how to study well. The time and effort you put in at first will lead to better learning, better grades, and more efficient use of study time. Since it does take some time to learn, you should start work on your study skills at the beginning of the school year, rather than wait until just before exams.

The first step in developing good study skills is setting up a study area in which you do nothing but study. This could be a special study room, a study desk, or a desk that you specifically rearrange just for study times. Using the principles of remove, avoid, and restrict from Chapter 5 (Change of Scene) make the study area as free from distractions as possible. Do not set up a study area in the midst of distracting people. A seat in the library where you do a lot of people-watching is not a good study area. Remove from the study area pictures, magazines, food, or anything else that might lead to something other than studying. In your study area have readily available all necessary equipment such as books, pencils, paper, and dictionary.

Do not do anything else in your study area but study. Do not daydream, sleep, write letters, or eat. Just study and try to keep it relaxed and pleasant. If you can't study and begin to daydream, feel discomfort, or something else incompatible with studying, then leave the study area. But don't reward yourself for leaving studying! Just take a short break and then return to studying. Save longer breaks and other rewards for when you finish a set amount of studying.

The second step in developing good study skills is setting goals. Decide in advance how much you will study each time. This might be based on the amount of material you will learn (not just read over) and/or the amount of time you will spend studying (not counting daydreaming etc.). Remember to take small steps: start with what you can do easily and gradually build up. Perhaps at first you can only study for 15 minutes. Fine, start there and study for 15 minutes in your study area and then take a break. Then gradually increase the amount of time you require yourself to study. You may find it useful to set different goals for different types of material. Thus your study goals when reading chemistry should be different than your study goals when drawing a figure. Make a graph of your progress in studying and post it where it is easily seen.

The third step is getting motivated. Here you want to be sure to include some of the procedures of Chapter 8 (Getting Motivated), such as rewarding yourself for gradually accomplishing your goals and setting up contracts with yourself about studying. Also make a list of reasons for studying, review this list occasionally, and add and subtract reasons along the way. You might wish to review this list each day before studying.

Be alert to things you say to yourself that keep you from studying and/or interfere with your studying. Review the procedures of Chapter 11 (What Do You Think) for ways to deal with troublesome thoughts.

The fourth step is developing <u>study habits</u>. Schedule your study times in advance, preferably times that do not conflict too much with other desirable activities. A daily calendar can be useful here. Spread out your studying over time, rather than cramming just before an exam. Learning is best when it is spread out. As much as possible, try to study at the same time each day. This helps develop a good habit of studying. Similarly try to do some studying each study day even if you don't have to. Study the least preferred material first before letting yourself study the more preferred material. Interrelate, compare, and contrast what you are learning with what you already know.

The fifth and final step is <u>observing your studying</u>. Know yourself: observe the way you act and think while studying. How focused is your attention? How well do you keep your mind on the material? Do you find you have read a page or two and don't remember what you read? Are you really studying or daydreaming? Are you trying to complete material rather than learn it? Do you skip over hard material and act as if you know it? Are you creating interest in what you are learning or creating disinterest or bad feelings? Are you distorting what you read to suit your biases?

Observe yourself. Be truthful with yourself about yourself. This will help you know what you need to do to further improve your study skills. Perhaps you will need to develop more concentration or perhaps you will have to work on some of your biases or perhaps....

SQ3R

Finally we consider the SQ3R method, a way to go through material you are studying. This is a highly researched, effective method of studying that helps both good students and poor students. SQ3R stands for

survey, question, read, recite, and review. It takes
a little time to master the SQ3R method and use it well,
but the time spent is well worth it for improving studying. You might first practice SQ3R on books and magazines you read for pleasure.

The first step is to briefly overview whatever
reading you are going to do. In the case of a book,
read the preface, look at the table of contents, and
skim over the book. Then break down the reading into
study units, such as chapters of a book,sections of a
long and difficult chapter, or individual articles.
Then apply SQ3R to one unit at a time in the following
sequence.

Survey. For a few minutes survey the unit of
material to be read. Glance over headings, look at
pictures and graphs, and read any summaries.

Question. Ask yourself questions about the material you surveyed and write the questions down. Make
up questions based on headings, concluding paragraphs,
and summaries. Ask other questions, such as why did
the instructor assign this reading? Review any questions in the material, such as questions at the end of
the chapter.

Read. Read through the unit, reading everything.
Answer your questions while reading. The first time
through, just read and answer questions. Then go back,
read it again, and underline important things.

Recite. This is one of the most important steps.
After you have read the material, put it away and from
memory summarize the general points giving examples.
You might write down a brief outline from memory. Then
go back through your questions and give answers from
memory.

Now go back and read again. Then put away the
material and recite again. Only now in recite, try to
recall what you have read and imagine explaining it to
someone else. Continue to read and recite until you
know the material.

Review. Next put away all notes and everything
and try to remember the main points. Then go over any
notes, underlinings, and headings and try to remember
subpoints to the main points. Finally reread briefly,
go over the headings, and review the main points.

There are many acceptable variations to the above SQ3R method. Do it as described above for a while and then find any variation that works best for you. For example, in one variation you use survey and review for large amounts of material (such as a long chapter) and use question, read, and recite for units of the material (such as sections of a chapter). Thus you might survey a whole chapter; question, read and recite the sections of the chapter; and then review the whole chapter.

But whatever approach you take, you can learn to study better if you <u>do</u> the things suggested in this chapter.

SUGGESTED READING

The suggested readings in this chapter are divided into three categories: memory, studying, and thinking.

MEMORY

These books discuss various ways to improve learning and memory and describe different mnemonic memory systems. The Bellezza, Lorayne & Lucas, and Markoff & Carcel books are perhaps best for the average reader. The books by Cermak and Higbee are more textbooks and go into other aspects of memory.

Bellezza, F. S. <u>Improve your memory skills</u>. Prentice-Hall, 1982.

Cermak, L. S. <u>Improving your memory</u>. McGraw-Hill, 1975.

Higbee, K. L. <u>Your memory: How it works and how to improve it</u>. Prentice-Hall, 1977.

Lorayne, H. & Lucas, J. <u>The memory book</u>. Stein & Day, 1974. Ballantine paperback, 1975.

Markoff, D. & Carcel, D. <u>Total recall</u>. Grosset & Dunlap, 1979. Charter Books paperback, 1979.

STUDYING

These are books written for college students on various aspects of student life including studying, taking exams, writing papers, and managing time.

Annis. L. F. <u>Study techniques</u>. Wm. C. Brown Co., 1983.

Locke, E. A. <u>A guide to effective study</u>. Springer, 1975.

Morgan, C. T. & Deese, J. <u>How to study</u>. McGraw-Hill,

1969.

Walter, T. & Siebert A. Student success: How to be a better student and still have time for your friends. Holt, Rinehart, & Winston, 1981

Walter, T. & Siebert, A. The adult students' guide to success in college. Holt, Rinehart & Winston, 1982.

THINKING

The de Bono book is filled with ideas and exercises to develop more flexible and creative thinking. It is good to use with yourself and it is good for parents and teachers to use with children. The Raudsepp & Hough book provides games and puzzles to stimulate thinking and creativity. Gardner's book is a series of mathematical, logic, and word puzzles and facilitates creative approaches to problem solving.

de Bono, E. Lateral thinking: Creativity step by step. Harper & Row, 1970. Harper Colophon paperback, 1973.

Raudsepp, E. & Hough, G. P. Creative growth games. Harcourt, Brace, Jovanovich, 1977.

Gardner, M. Aha! Insight. W. H. Freeman, 1978.

CHAPTER TWENTY ONE

INTRODUCTION TO SECTION FOUR

Although the topics of this section may seem of a
different type than the topics of previous sections,
the more time and work you have spent on previous chapters the more you will profit from the next chapters.
The reason for this is that you must first have a good
start on getting your life under control and dealing
with problems of daily living before you can most prof-
itably work in more subtle areas such as freedom, happiness, and love. However, as you work on the next
topics, you should be continuing to work on previous
topics. In fact, work in the areas of this section
will help you see other things you may want to work
on using previous approaches.

The material in this section may be a little more
difficult because it suggests that you look at your
life in a somewhat different way and reconsider some
things you have always accepted but not really thought
about. Therefore you should read the chapters in this
section slowly and think about them carefully. Then
re-read the chapters. When you finally finish this
book, put it away for a while and then get it out and
read this section again.

SUGGESTED READING

Shapiro's book combines American behavioral self-
management with Zen Buddhism. This includes topics
such as relaxation, meditation, increased awareness,
freedom, yielding, and sense of self. For some people
this book would be a good transition from the previous
sections to the current section. Williams and Long's
book, written for college students, covers some of the
topics of previous sections, a little of the topics of
this section, and some topics not treated in this book.
Chapters include establishing social relationships,
working with groups, maintaining intimate relationships, managing stress, countering depression, dealing
with divorce, planning your career, acquiring a good
job, getting and giving help, and achieving personal
fulfillment, among others.

Shapiro, D. H. Precision nirvana. Prentice-Hall,
    1978.

175

Williams, R. L. & Long, J. D. _Toward a self-managed life style_. Houghton-Mifflin, 1983.

CHAPTER TWENTY TWO

PERSONAL FREEDOM

We all have basic rights to live our lives as we choose, as long as we don't interfere with the rights of others. Our society puts restrictions on us by way of laws, ethics, and social conventions. These restrictions are taught to us by our parents, teachers, friends, and religious groups, as well as by means of newspapers, books, television, and movies. Every society has and needs some types of restrictions in order to function well and best help the members of the society.

The problem is that with so many people telling us how to live, most of us end up with too many constraints on our freedom. And many of these constraints are unnecessary and/or undesirable. The world is filled with so many wonderful things to do and experience. We miss out on a lot if we are not free and making choices. You can be a lot freer (more free) than you are now. This chapter tells how.

Now becoming freer does not mean becoming irresponsible, eccentric, troublesome, or law-breaking (although you may become one of these if you choose to). Rather, if you wish your life to be the most effective and happy, you must assume responsibility for your life. This means responsibility for everything you do, say, and think and how these influence your world and other people. When you are totally responsible for your life, you can reconsider some of the constraints on your freedom.

BECOMING FREER

The first step to becoming freer is to learn to identify the constraints on you. It is another example of know yourself. Practice being aware of various social pressures for you to do something or not do something. Identify the source of the constraint, such as social custom, family ethics, or pressure from friends.

The second step is to question the constraint, even if it seems obvious. Does it make sense? Is it right? Should it apply to you? If it once applied to you, does it still apply? Should you do it just because everybody else does?

The last step is to choose a course of action that frees you from those constraints that are unnecessary and/or undesirable. The course of action must be a responsible choice as it affects you and others. Be sure to consider the practical effects of whatever you do. If you decide you are going to quit the woman's club, stop mowing your yard, grow a beard, or go back to school at age 60, be aware of how this will affect other people and how they will then act toward you.

But freedom is not simply breaking free of constraints. Freedom is the <u>realization</u> that you may go along with the constraints or you may not. Freedom is having the choice!! A person who is influenced by his friends to do something he would prefer not to do, is not free. A person who chooses to go along with his friends is free. The totally free person is <u>aware</u> of the many constraints on her or him,<u>chooses</u> to go along with most or all of the constraints since they are appropriate, and <u>chooses</u> to be free or unaffected by those constraints which are not appropriate. The free and responsible person chooses to do those things she has a legitimate duty to do.

However, having the freedom to choose a course of action does not mean you have the skills to accomplish your goals. The purpose of this book is to provide you with some of these skills. Thus you have the freedom to choose not to be overweight, but may need the technology of an earlier chapter to do it.

<u>SIMPLE EXAMPLES</u>
The following are some examples of common constraints that many people could break free from.

You do not have to jog or play tennis, even though it is good for you and all your friends are doing it. Perhaps you will choose to play more tennis because you decide you want the exercise. But you don't have to do it because people tell you to.

You do not have to keep up with the news. You do not have to watch the news on television. You do not have to subscribe to a news magazine. You do not have to know about world affairs. You may decide that you wish or should follow the news; but the choice is yours. An an exercise, disregard the news for a week or two.

You may celebrate your birthday, Christmas, or any

other holiday on any day of the year you want. For example, one year it may work out better for you to celebrate Thanksgiving on Saturday, not Thursday. I was born on December 27, which is still my legal birthday. But for many years I have celebrated the occasion of my birth in September when it better fits my life and is not so close to Christmas.

You do not have to answer the phone when it rings. Why should someone dialing a mechanical device require you to stop what you are doing and go talk on the phone? There are times when being responsible makes it necessary to answer the phone. But there are also times when you should not answer, times when you need to be alone or times when you are doing something that shouldn't be interrupted. As an exercise, try not answering the phone a few times when you don't need to.

When you are on a vacation you do not have to do what others think you should do. If you want to spend your vacation working in your garden, bowling, or going to a meditation retreat, it is your choice. If you go somewhere on your vacation you do not have to see certain things just because they are common tourist sights. If you go to France, you do not have to go to Paris and see the Eiffel tower, unless you want to. In fact you do not even have to go to Paris; you might prefer to stay in villages. On the other hand, if you want to see many common tourist attractions, that is fine.

Remember, in terms of freedom it is having the choice which is important, not what you choose. In terms of responsibility it is what you choose that is important. The above examples are not saying what you should do, but are situations in which you have a choice.

PERSONAL FREEDOM
When increasing your own personal freedom one of the biggest obstacles is "should." On every side there is someone to tell you what you should do. Your conscience, based on what people have told you in the past, is ready to tell you what you should do. But the fact that you are being told what you should do does not mean this is the best thing to do. Perhaps the "should" is based on ethical ideas that you do not hold. Or perhaps the "should" was applicable when you were a child, but no longer applies. See Chapter 11 (What Do You Think) for a discussion of how to evaluate and perhaps change thoughts, such as "should" thoughts, that may be

irrational and/or undesirable.

Another obstacle to personal freedom is the concern about being wrong. Many people put constraints
on themselves rather than admit being wrong. Thus a
person will continually act or think in some way
rather than see he is wrong and change the way he acts
or thinks. Thus he constrains himself. The free person can see and admit she is wrong and then she has the
freedom to choose what she will do next. Everybody
makes mistakes. You often learn best from mistakes.
You have the right to be wrong. You have the right to
change your mind. You just must be responsible.

Maybe there is a person you don't like and you
have a lot of good reasons for not liking him. Well,
maybe he has changed or maybe you were wrong in some
of your impressions or facts. No problem. You are not
a victim of the past. What are you going to do now?
You have the freedom to let the past go and now like
the person. You also have the freedom to still dislike the person. It is your choice. But be sure it
is a free choice and you are not constraining yourself
with your own past.

Maybe there is a social or political position you
have advocated in the past. Perhaps many people know
you held this position. But you do not have to hold
this position any longer if you don't want. You are
free. You can change your mind. You can be wrong.
Everybody who continually improves his life must occasionally take new roads and leave the past behind.

You have the right not to understand. The intelligent person often says "I do not know" and "I don't
understand that." The less intelligent person pretends
he understands things he doesn't understand, which often
leads to problems.

You have the right not to care. You do not have
to care about or be concerned about something because
you are told you should. You have a responsibility to
care about many things, but not everything you are told
to care about. The world is filled with things you
could care about; but you can only care about a small
fraction of them. You must make some decisions; you
must have some priorities; you do have the freedom.

You have the right to form and express your own
beliefs. You have the responsibility to see and under-

stand things as best you can. You have the right to
say how things seem to you and express how you feel.
When you and your associates exercise these rights and
respect them in each other, you have laid the ground-
work for good communication, problem-solving, and maximizing each person's potential.

You have the freedom to choose however you wish
to feel. You may think that your feelings are forced
on you by various situations. This is true for most
people. But you have the freedom to choose how you
feel. Then it becomes a question of how to do it. Earlier chapters have covered how to control various feelings, such as anxiety and desires for food or cigarettes. And the next chapter covers how to be happy.
The choice is up to you.

Remember, everyone can be freer than he or she
is. Discovering constraints on your freedom is something you can do right now. Then once you get this
process started and keep at it, for many years you
will find more and more undesirable constraints. The
process will take you to subtler and subtler levels
of your being and you will become freer and freer in
ways that will bring you greater pleasure, clearer
perceptions, improved thinking, and better interactions
with your world and other people.

SUGGESTED READING

The first three books by Browne, Dyer, and Maul &
Maul will help you identify some of the obstacles to
your own freedom. They also suggest ways to overcome
these obstacles. You need not agree with everything
these authors suggest, but you will profit from their
help in evaluating your own freedom. The last four
books are for the person who needs to be more assertive. These are for the person who could use some
help in standing up for his rights and expressing what
he thinks and feels. The assertive person is one who
has found the effective and appropriate middleground
between being too unassertive and being too aggressive.

Browne, H. How I found freedom in an unfree world.
    Macmillan, 1973. Avon paperback, 1974.
Dyer, W. W. Your erroneous zones. Funk and Wagnalls,
    1976. Avon paperback, 1977.
Maul, G. & Maul, T. Beyond limit: Ways to growth
    and freedom. Scott Foresman, 1983.

Alberti, R. E. & Emmons, M. L. Stand up, speak out, talk back. Pocket book paperback, 1975.

Jakubowski, P. & Lange, A. J. The assertive option. Research Press, 1978.

Dyer, W. W. Pulling your own strings. Crowell, 1978. Avon paperback, 1979.

Baer, J., How to be an assertive (not aggressive) woman in life, in love, and on the job. Signet paperback, 1976.

CHAPTER TWENTY-THREE

HAPPINESS

Most people would list happiness or becoming happier as a major goal for their lives. But most people go about it in entirely the wrong way. Fortunately there is a specific path that will lead you to greater happiness and peace of mind. This chapter describes that path, a path which is easy to understand, takes some work and time, and continually simplifies your life and brings more happiness.

For discussion we use the words "pleasure" and "happiness" in specific ways. By "pleasure" is meant a short-lived state or feeling due to an enjoyable event or activity. Eating something you like is a source of pleasure. It stimulates your taste, vision, and sense of smell. It thus provides pleasure for a while. Later a memory of it may be a source of pleasure. The opposite of pleasure is pain. By "happiness" is meant the longer term satisfaction you have with your life. Overall, how content are you with your life and the world you live in?

SOURCES OF PLEASURE

There are many potential sources of pleasure. Some primarily stimulate your senses, such as tasting a good drink, seeing a beautiful sunset or a pleasing work of art, and feeling the body pleasure of exercise or sex. Other sources of pleasure are social, such as the pleasure that may come from recognition, approval, or accomplishment. Some sources of pleasure are mental and arise with pleasant memories and thoughts and with new ideas and understanding. And there is the pleasure that goes with improving your life, getting rid of obstacles, learning new skills, quieting your mind, and moving on the path of happiness.

Stop and think about the sources of pleasure in your life. Make a list of those things which are the most pleasurable to you. After making your list, think about whether you consider it undesirable that any particular thing on your list gives you pleasure. If so, what can you do about it, as with the techniques in this book?

YOUR HAPPINESS

Consider your whole life, including your health,

work, family, friends, home, possessions, and everything else. How happy are you with your life? Always be totally honest with yourself: are you happy all of the time? most of the time? some of the time? little of the time? almost never?

Make a list of the things you would need or like in order to be much happier. After making the list, spend some time thinking about how you would have answered this question differently at different ages of your life, such as when you were 5, 12, 17, 23 etc. That is, when you were 5 what would you have said you wanted or needed in order to be very happy? What would you have said at other ages? We will come back to this list a little later.

PLEASURE AND HAPPINESS

Pleasure is one of the main sources of happiness for most people. Thus a person can often increase his happiness by increasing his pleasure. People who have little pleasure in their lives should seek out new activities, people, clubs, services, and so forth. The world is filled with sources of pleasure for everyone.

Many people think happiness is primarily based on pleasure and thus try to be happy by continually seeking pleasure. But this does not work very well at all, for pleasure does not last and what is pleasurable today may not be pleasurable tomorrow. So people who are too caught up in pleasure spend a lot of time seeking pleasure, worrying about the next source of pleasure, and trying to hold on to things that bring pleasure. But this just brings a craving for pleasure, not happiness!

One reason that craving for pleasure is not a good route to happiness is the universal fact that everything changes. Something that brought you pleasure before will change and perhaps lose some of its pleasure to you. Thus a restaurant, a vacation place, a game, or a friendship changes and may become less pleasing. Many people try to prevent this by keeping things from changing or pretending they are not changing; but this will not work well in the long run. Everything changes. A person who fails to honestly recognize the changes in his business organization and pretends things have not changed is clinging to a false sense of pleasure and hurting his own perceptions, effectiveness, and happiness. A parent who doesn't allow a child enough space to grow and change hurts both himself and the child.

You change and what is pleasurable to you changes. If
you cling to certain pleasures, you limit the changes
in yourself and thus limit your potential for other
pleasures and greater happiness. If every time you went
out to eat you ordered the same thing, you may maintain
some pleasure. But you would be missing out on a lot,
including other pleasures and a happiness greater than
pleasure. All of life is a great banquet. Don't fall
for the trap of believing that happiness is found by
clinging to a few sources of pleasure. Everything, including you, should and does change.

Many people seek happiness through the pleasure
of possessions. Such people continually get newer and
"better" clothes, stereos, cars, houses, or whatever.
One problem with this clinging to possessions is that
the possessions use up a lot of your time and money.
Possessions have to be cleaned, repaired, kept up, used,
insured, and then replaced. Pay attention to how much
of your time and energy is tied into your possessions.
Are you possessed by possessions?

A second problem with possessions as a source of
pleasure, which is a problem with many sources of pleasure, is the trap of <u>more is never enough</u>. As long as
you believe you need <u>more</u> of something to be happy, you
will never get enough. People who think all they need
is more money to be happy will always desire more, no
matter how much they have. And thus they limit their
own happiness. The person whose interest and hobby is
music equipment might be pretty happy with his current
turntable, amplifiers, speakers, and so forth. But,
he believes he will really be happy when he finally
gets.... So he always wants more.

More is never enough is such a common trap that
everyone falls for it in one way or another. Everyone!
Everyone believes he will be significantly happier as
soon as he has more friends, more power, or more something. Carefully watch for when you fall into this
trap. Learning to avoid this trap is a critical and
very powerful part of the path to happiness. Remember:
<u>More is never enough</u>. Enough is always enough.

So pleasure can be one source of things that increases our happiness. But clinging to pleasure or
continually seeking more is not a good approach to
happiness. Happiness is much broader. In fact, happiness does not depend on pleasure! You can be happy
with pleasure, without pleasure, and even with pain.

How to do this is discussed below. But first we must consider some more of what does not work.

WHAT DOESN'T WORK
Earlier in this chapter you made a list of what you want or need to be happy. Let us now look at the list. (If you haven't yet made the list, go back and do it now.)

How many of the things on the list were things of pleasure? What does this tell you? How many were possessions? What does this tell you?

Most people when making such a happiness list put down things related to money, power, fame, recognition, family, friends, and health, among other things. People say things such as:I'll be really happy as soon as I find a good husband. As soon as I am promoted I'll be happy. If I had $100,000 I could get everything I need to be happy. I'll be happy as soon as I finish school and get a good job. What is on your list?

But none of these will bring significant lasting happiness. They may bring some pleasure and some happiness; but they miss the fundamental nature of happiness. Consider money. Certainly the people with the most money are not the happiest. In fact, on the average, they are less happy than similar people without the wealth. For money can cause many problems such as a loss of value of other things, anxiety and concern about protecting the money, and the more is never enough trap. Or consider people with a lot of fame or power, people such as movie stars and politicians. These people have not found more total happiness in fame or power than other people have found in other things. Many famous and powerful people suffer myriads of personal problems. The divorce rate among movie stars is very high. Many politicians suffer the stress of their work.

Next consider how at different ages you would have answered the question of what you want or need to be happy. One person at 5 believed that all he needed was a new bicycle to be totally happy. Another person at 14 was convinced a driver's license was the key to happiness. At 17 another person believed marriage was the way. What did you think at different ages? Now the fact is that none of these actually worked to the degree expected. For when he got the bicycle it brought

him a lot of pleasure at first and then some lasting
pleasure. But after a while he was not as happy as he
wanted to be. Now to be happy he needed.... When the
person finally got his driver's license, he was very
excited and pleased. And driving has added to his
pleasure ever since. But the driver's license was not
the key to happiness, for he soon decided that to be
really happy he wanted....

And so it goes for everyone. Each person pursues
happiness by expecting to be much happier when he
achieves some possession, age, position, goal, or the
types of things discussed above. And this pursuit
works to some degree. But when the person reaches his
goal (e.g., owns the bike, gets married, is promoted),
he finds he is not as happy as he expected, for soon
there are other things that are needed or wanted for
happiness. So everybody finds that much or most of
happiness keeps being just out of reach. Most people
spend their lives pursuing happiness, perhaps feeling
they are close to it, but never fully getting a hold
of it. Put a lot of thought to this and how it relates
to you and to what you listed would make you happy.
What has been described is true for everybody, in different ways. So don't be alarmed if it is true for
you.

Consider a hard-working farming family of two
thousand years ago. Suppose someone described to them
the following: They would be freed of most of the
diseases that bothered and killed them. They would
live in a weather-proof home that automatically controlled the temperature to their taste. Machines would
cook their food, wash their dishes, and wash and dry
their clothes. Another machine would bring all sorts
of entertainment into their home and show them live
scenes from around the world. Simply by dialing numbers on another piece of equipment they could talk to
friends miles away. Another miraculous device would
carry them wherever they wanted to go, smoothly traveling along roads in a weather-proof box. We could add
many more examples here. The point is that to this
family of the past (or many families of our world today)
all of this sounds quite wonderful. They might easily
believe that anyone who had all of these things would
have to be very happy. But the fact is that many American families have all of this and are not very happy.

Now this does not mean there is anything "wrong"
with possessions, money, fame, various sources of

187

pleasure, or any of the other goals mentioned above. A
person should continue to have personal goals for his
life, including goals that will bring pleasure. But
clinging to any of these sources of pleasure or goals
as the way to real happiness is following a path that
leads you on, but you never get to where you want.
Happiness, in a much broader and more significant sense,
is found another way, discussed next.

WHAT DOES WORK
        The key to happiness is very basic: Develop
unconditional acceptance for reality as it is. Be
accepting of every situation you are in. This does
not mean having no preferences or opinions. It does
not mean being wishy-washy or fatalistic. It does not
mean giving up your values or ethics. You should still
do what you think is best. You should still try to influence people and situations in the direction you believe is right. You should still do the best you can
with each situation, acting with responsibility, precision, respect, and pleasure.

        But after you have done what you can do, you should
accept things as they are. Reality can only be as it
is, not as it is not. To make yourself unhappy because
reality is what it is, not the way you want it to be
or think it should be, is a losing strategy. You only
hurt yourself and decrease your own happiness by thinking this way. Do your best and accept things as they
are.

        This does not mean you have to like the situation
you are now accepting (that would be confusing pleasure
with happiness). And it does not mean you won't try to
make things different in the future. But while you are
doing whatever you do, accept things as they are. Accept
them unconditionally, that is, with no qualifications.

        Cultivating unconditional acceptance of reality
as it is will be for you the path to happiness, a very
basic happiness that is more complete and more satisfying than happiness sought after by other means.
Developing this happiness will also provide you with
much more pleasure than you would attain by chasing
after and clinging to sources of pleasure. And cultivating unconditional acceptance will also make you more
effective at whatever you do.

        What most people do is compare things the way they
are with the way they want things to be or think they

should be. Then if there is a difference, they make
themselves unhappy. This approach is the major obstacle to happiness, for there will almost always be
a difference and hence unhappiness. Even if a person
gets things so there is little or no difference, this
won't last because everything changes. There is a
universal tendency for people to fall into this trap
of making themselves unhappy because their model of
how reality should be doesn't match reality as it is.
Spiritual teachers throughout the ages have pointed
out the importance of avoiding this trap.

     To avoid the trap you simply do your best and cul-
tivate unconditional acceptance for how things are.
Reinhold Neibuhr offered the following prayer: "God
grant me the serenity to accept the things I can not
change; the courage to change the things I can; and the
wisdom to know the difference."

     For example, you and some friends are going out
to the beach with a picnic lunch. Then when you get
out there it is raining such that you don't leave the
car. Gone are your plans of lying in the sun. Gone
are your hopes of sitting by the water with wine and
cheese. What could have turned out to be a nice time
has fallen apart. You certainly aren't happy about all
of this. But you have made yourself unhappy. Why make
yourself upset because the weather is not the way you
expected or wanted it to be? The weather is as it is.
You can still be very happy if you can let go of your
plans, expectations, wants, and shoulds. It can be an
exciting, pleasurable time to sit in your car and watch
the rain over the water. And you can do this while
sharing a nice picnic lunch with your good friends. In
fact you might have really looked forward to this if
your friends had come by, told you it was raining at
the beach, and suggested you take a picnic lunch and
watch the rain on the water from your car.

     As another example, your daughter is living with
someone in a relationship you disapprove of. Now you
certainly have a responsibility as a parent and friend
of your daughter to discuss your concerns with her. But
after you have done whatever you think you should do,
it would be foolish to make yourself unhappy or mad
because things are not the way you want. Keep doing
whatever you decide to do. But don't get upset because reality doesn't match your wants and shoulds. In
fact, getting upset in this situation will hurt your
relationship with your daughter and impair your thinking

and communication with her.

In the game of life you win some and you lose some. Winning may provide some pleasure and losing may cause some pain; but happiness is not found in the winning or losing. Happiness is found in how you play the game. You do your best to win and enjoy the related pleasure. You realize you will sometimes lose and you have interest in what you experience when losing. You unconditionally accept both winning and losing as part of the game. You become happy just playing the game. And later, winning and losing become much less important. You are having too much fun just playing.

YOU ARE RESPONSIBLE

So it turns out that you are totally responsible for how happy you are. People and events may be related to your pleasure and pain, but not to your happiness. It is your acceptance of the people and events which affects your happiness. If somebody says or does something which upsets you, then (1) do or say whatever is appropriate to the situation, (2) do not blame the other person for upsetting you, and (3) assume responsibility for being upset and do something about it.

Another person may be partly responsible for something he did that hurt you in the past. But if you now remember it and get upset, you are totally responsible for your current feelings.

BECOMING HAPPIER

Consider the following points dealing with how to become happier, as discussed above.
1. Relax body and mind. Learn how to relax your body and quiet your mind (Chapter 6). Develop a relaxed living style (Chapter 7).

2. Work on specific problems. Work out programs to deal with specific problem areas that impair happiness, such as some desires (Chapter 10) and some fears (Chapter 15).

3. Get pleasure under control. Find ways to add desirable pleasures to your life. Get free from undesirable pleasures. Do not cling to pleasure as a means to happiness.

4. Work with your thoughts. The things you tell yourself can be a major cause of unhappiness. Observe your thoughts and replace negative thinking with posi-

190

tive thinking (Chapter 11).

5. Observe your unhappiness. When you are not
happy is an excellent time to see why you aren't happy
and what you can do about it. For example, if you are
not as happy as you could be, see if it is because
you are comparing reality as it is with your model of
how it should be or you want it to be.

6. Cultivate unconditional acceptance. This, of
course, is the key: learning to unconditionally accept
reality as it is. This will take time and work. So
remember our strategy of taking small steps. Some
situations will be easy to accept: enjoy the pleasure
here. Some situations will take some effort to accept:
these are the situations where you have an opportunity
to improve and increase your happiness. Some situations
you are not capable of accepting: let these go for now.
Unconditional acceptance includes accepting yourself as
and where you are, and then moving on.

7. Be patient. This is a gradual process that
can't be rushed.

BEYOND HAPPINESS
As you become more accepting you will become happier, more loving, and more aware. You will find that
the real you is not your body or your mind. As you
gradually discover the real you, you will become less
vulnerable. For the pleasures and pains of your body
and your mind need not affect your happiness; they are
not you. All of the sensations, thoughts, memories,
desires,and conflicts are the working of your mind. But
you are not your mind. So you observe and work with
these processes of your mind, but they are not you.
Even happiness itself is a state of mind. As you further cultivate unconditional acceptance it leads you
past happiness to peace of mind, a place of total experience with a sense of total freedom.

But the first step is to work with pleasure, happiness, and unconditional acceptance. You now know
what you can do to make your life as happy as you want.
It is now up to you. What are you going to do now?

SUGGESTED READING

The Handbook to Higher Consciousness is a useful
manual for identifying and overcoming obstacles

("addictions") to happiness, love, and conscious growth. The book is somewhat based on principles from the human potential movement, Buddhism, and yoga. To Love is to be Happy With emphasizes learning to be happy with life as it is. This involves questioning what makes you unhappy, why that makes you unhappy, what beliefs you have about happiness, and what you are afraid would happen if you weren't unhappy. How to Stop Worrying and Start Living contains a lot of useful advice on how to worry less. Many topics are covered including analyzing the situation, co-operating with the inevitable, positive thinking, the use of prayer, dealing with criticism, and finding a vocation. How to Love Every Minute of Your Life discusses getting in touch with and dealing with your feelings, including those related to interpersonal relationships, communication, and sex. There are also chapters on parents and children and being single. Be the Person You Were Meant to Be is based on gestalt therapy and involves moving from behavior that is emotionally "toxic" (impairs natural functioning, happiness, and personal growth) to behavior that is emotionally "nourishing." 2150 uses a science fiction format to discuss "Macro Philosophy" which includes the statement, "The measure of a mind's evolution is its acceptance of the unacceptable." The Conquest of Happiness is an essay by a noted philosopher on the causes of unhappiness (e.g., competition, boredom, envy) and the causes of happiness (e.g., zest affection, work). He includes some practical suggestions, such as developing a wide range of interests and cultivating friendly and affectionate relations.

Keyes, Jr., K. Handbook to higher consciousness. Living Love Publications, 5th edition, 1975.
Kaufman, B. N. To love is to be happy with. Fawcett Crest paperback, 1977.
Carnegie, D. How to stop worrying and start living. Simon & Schuster, 1948. Pocket Book paperback, 1953.
Hendricks, G. & Leavenworth, C. How to love every minute of your life. Prentice-Hall, 1978.
Greenwald, J. Be the person you were meant to be. Simon & Schuster, 1973. Dell paperback, 1974.
Alexander, T. 2150. Warner Books paperback, 1976.
Russell, B. The conquest of happiness. Liveright, 1930. Avon paperback.

CHAPTER TWENTY-FOUR

LOVE

What does it mean when you say you love someone? Does it mean respect or admiration? Does it include desire or sexual attraction? Is it partially based on common interests or fulfilling each other's needs? Or is love something different or more than these?

Most people's love relationships with other people are largely based on components such as those mentioned above. Thus when Al says he loves June, it really means he is sexually attracted to June; she feeds some of his needs by giving him emotional support when he feels insecure; and they enjoy doing many of the same things. Similarly, when June says she loves Al, it really means Al fits her image of how a male partner should be; he provides the security that she needs, and he treats her much nicer than other men she has been involved with. Now these examples are much simpler than are real life cases, but they illustrate what most love relationships are built on.

However, these components are usually not a good basis for a long term relationship, because <u>everything changes</u>. Sue primarily got married for security and because it was the thing to do. However, after a few years when her other needs were more important than her need for security, she found that the marriage was no longer satisfying. For years Bob loved his son, Brad. Brad was cute, interesting, and fun to be with. Bob and Brad would do many things together that Bob had always wanted to do with his father. However, as Brad got older he became more of an individual and wanted to spend less time with Bob. Brad also started acting in ways Bob didn't expect and often didn't like. Soon Bob found he didn't love his son as much as he had before.

Fortunately there can be much more to love than has been discussed so far. Love can exist and grow regardless of needs and desires and expectations. Love can help a person find the most fulfilling life possible. Love can help two people merge in heart and spirit as they go through life together or go separate ways. Love can open the heart, expand the mind, and overcome unwanted emotions such as anger and fear.

The rest of this chapter shows you basic ways to develop this most powerful form of love.

UNCONDITIONAL ACCEPTANCE
The idea of unconditional acceptance was introduced in the last chapter on happiness. You should have read that chapter carefully before continuing on here.

Optimal love of any other person involves unconditional acceptance of that person. If you love a person, you should try to accept and love that person no matter what the person does. Unconditional means no matter what. You may disagree with the person, but you still love him or her. You may try to change the way a person thinks or acts, but you love unconditionally. You may punish a child for misbehavior, but you love the child the same no matter what.

The key to this is to realize that you can love a person regardless of whether you like or dislike how that person behaves. A person is not his behavior. If you dislike a person's behavior, do something about it if you can. But love the person regardless. Love requires unconditional acceptance of a person no matter how the person behaves. Your love for another person should only grow regardless of what he does, in sickness or in health, for better or for worse. Unconditional acceptance. Through love you create space for the other person to grow, learn, and approach or withdraw.

LOVE YOURSELF UNCONDITIONALLY
The first person for you to love unconditionally is yourself. This often turns out to be very hard. Most people are their own worst critics and are not very accepting of themselves. You will spend your whole life with you; so you should make good friends with yourself.

Again, this does not mean that you should like everything that you do; but you should always try to unconditionally accept and love yourself. As you observe the way you act, think, and feel, you may find many things you want to change. Fine. Do something about it. That is what this book is about. But while all this is going on, love and accept yourself unconditionally. Perhaps you are a disorganized, neurotic, alcoholic and don't like being that way. Well, if you don't like it, do something about it. But always love yourself. Love yourself as a person whose life situations led to being a disorganized, neurotic, alcoholic. Love yourself as a person who doesn't like being this way. Love yourself when you try to do something about your life. Love yourself when you mess up. Love yourself when you make progress. No matter what you do, you always love yourself unconditionally.

Perhaps you will find yourself in a situation in which you feel you can't love yourself or you don't know how to love yourself. Fine. Simply love yourself as a person who is having trouble loving himself or herself. See, there is no way out. You should always love and accept yourself unconditionally as best you can, and then love yourself for doing the best you can.

Loving yourself unconditionally does not mean fooling yourself. Be totally honest. See yourself as you <u>are</u>. Accept and love yourself as you <u>are</u>. Then change anything you think needs changing.

LOVING OTHERS

Your life will become better in many ways as you learn to love other people unconditionally. This means <u>all</u> other people, not just the people you have close relationships with, not just the people you like, not just the people you know well, but all other people. Again, this does not mean you have to like the way another person acts. You may not like the person's behavior and you may try to help the person change his behavior. But regardless of how the person behaves, you love him or her as a person. Love and accept everyone unconditionally. Through love you will find glory and pleasure in how individuals differ, rather than trying to force people into molds.

Loving everyone unconditionally is very hard and will take some work. Remember our principle of taking small steps. At first some people will be easy to love and others will seem impossible to love. Simply start where you are and love as much as you can. And, of course, continually love yourself all this time. As you practice loving people more and more, the strength of your love will grow. After a while you will be loving people you could not love before, even if you don't like the way they behave. As your love grows, boundaries between you and others will fall away and your whole world will open and blossom. Eventually you will be able to love your enemies as you love your-

195

self, as Christ recommended.

A good way to learn to love another person is to try to see the world from his or her point of view. Just about everyone is trying to do what he or she thinks is best to do, according to his or her understanding and values. There are no good or bad people. There is only us, a bunch of people whose life experiences have led them to doing different things, seeing and thinking in different ways, and doing the best they can. To love other people try to see as they see, think as they think, and feel as they feel. Experience their joy and pain. What would it be like if you had another person's limitations or obstacles to overcome? Role-reversal, discussed at the end of Chapter 12 (Mental Rehearsal) may be useful here. Try to see everyone as your equal and love them unconditionally.

There is no particular way you must act as you love more. Developing unconditional love for others does not mean you must become more emotional, hug people more, tell more people you love them, or have certain loving looks on your face. You may do any of these you wish, but that is not the point. Love is more basic than just the way you look and act. Love is not necessarily sentimental. Love is a compassionate creating of space and support for others to grow and learn to love more. As you become more loving your whole being will reflect your love. As you become more unconditionally accepting of others, it will naturally lead to the most appropriate way to act.

As you learn to love yourself and others more you will find your life filled with much more happiness and pleasure. You will find you develop more meaningful and lasting relationships with others, including friendships and relationships that are part sexual. And you will be better able to communicate with others, really hearing what they mean and best conveying your thoughts and feelings.

AGGRESSION
The opposite of love is hate. Hate impairs your thinking and perception. Hate decreases your happiness and puts stress on your body. Hate builds barriers between you and others. Hate is only destructive; it is never desirable. Hate breeds more hate. You can not overcome hate with hate, in yourself or in someone else. Hate always increases hate. Only love decreases hate. You decrease the hate in your

196

world by increasing your love.

Even if you do not have much hate in your life, you still want to avoid anything which moves toward hate and away from love. One of the most common feelings to avoid is aggression, a tendency to attack. It might involve physically hurting a person, animal, or something else. It might involve hurting a person's feelings by what you say or do, or by what you don't say or do. Aggression comes in many forms: a verbal attack, bringing up a person's weak points or sore spots, pushing for your ideas without adequately considering others' ideas, or looking to blame others for what is your responsibility. Aggression is a move toward hate and away from love.

Thus it is to your advantage to decrease any feelings of aggression toward others, toward yourself, toward things, or toward ideas. Decreasing your _feelings_ of aggression does not mean that you must _behave_ in a very passive manner. There may arise situations in your life in which it is appropriate for you to take a strong position, stand up for what you believe, keep from being pushed around or defend yourself. That is, there may be times when it is appropriate for you to _behave_ in a strong or assertive manner. But it is not desirable for you to _feel_ aggressive during these times. If your child misbehaves, you may wish to correct your child; but you don't want to feel aggressive to him or her. If you are trying to influence people at a meeting, it may be good to speak with strong convictions and concerns; but it is not good to do it from aggressive feelings. Doing things while feeling aggressive always makes you less effective at whatever you are doing.

Practice being more aware of when you start to feel, think, or act in an aggressive way. When you see this occur, try, as best you can, to relax your body and mind. Try to be more relaxed and more loving. Treat each tendency to become aggressive as a signal to you that you have just hit one of the obstacles to your own happiness and love. See what causes your aggression and do something about it. Relax and love.

Gradually learn not to be upset when someone acts aggressively toward you. When someone is being aggressive, it is usually because he is in some sort of trouble. He may be afraid or insecure or defending a position he is unsure of. He might not know what to

197

do or what is right. People are usually aggressive
when they are weak and hurt. So if a person is aggressive to you, don't hurt yourself by letting yourself become aggressive, angry, or anxious. Rather see
the other person as someone in trouble. Be compassionate and loving. Maybe you can help him.

If a person is aggressive to you, handle the aggression in whatever way is appropriate, which may involve your taking a strong stand. But don't let another person's aggression make you aggressive. Instead,
love other people unconditionally.

Be concerned that you do not offend others, rather
than that you are not offended. Have as your goal the
resolving of conflict, rather than the gaining of advantage.

As you decrease aggression and increase unconditional acceptance and love, you will transform your
life in ways you desire. Start now! Good things are
in store for you.

SUGGESTED READING

Buscaglia, L. Love. Charles B. Slack, 1972.
    Fawcett Crest paperback.
Fromm, E. The art of loving. Harper & Row, 1956.
Hendricks, G. Learning to love yourself. Prentice-
    Hall, 1982.

CHAPTER TWENTY-FIVE

INNER PEACE

In Chapter 23 you learned about happiness: how to
increase your happiness, how to identify and avoid some
common traps that prevent happiness, and how to begin
to develop unconditional acceptance. Chapter 24 continued some of these ideas and there you learned how
to further develop unconditional acceptance and love
for yourself and others. After you have spent a lot
of time working with the ideas of these two chapters,
you are ready to move on to learning about inner peace.

Learning how to control your happiness is very
important, for you are responsible for your own happiness. But happiness is just a state of mind. As you
develop unconditional acceptance even more it will lead
you to an inner peace and freedom in which you are always satisfied, even if you aren't happy.

Learning to love more is critical. You can not
reach the full potential of your living if you don't
love enough. As you love more and more it will also
open to you this inner peace. To understand how to
further develop inner peace consider the idea of cen-
tering.

YOUR CENTER
Deep within you is a calm, quiet, peaceful center.
When you are in this center you are relaxed and aware.
You are free from confusion. Your perceptions are
direct and accurate and your mind is clear and effec-
tive.

You are not your body. Your body is part of everything you observe from your center. You may decide to
help or change your body. You are not your feelings
and emotions. These are part of everything you observe from your center. You may decide to change some
of your feelings or emotions. You are not your behavior. The way you talk and act is part of everything
you observe from your center. You may decide to change
some of your behavior. You are not your mind or
thoughts. Your specific thoughts and the processes of
your mind are part of everything you observe from your
center. You may decide to change how or what you think.

When you are centered (in your center), you are

clearly and peacefully observing everything you do.
You are a witness of your feelings, thoughts, and behavior. This witness does not judge or evaluate what
it sees. The mind evaluates and the witness observes
the mind. The witness does not emotionally react. Your
body and mind have feelings and emotions; the witness
observes all this.

When you are centered, the real you can not be
hurt. Your body can be hurt; but that's not you. Your
feelings can be hurt; but they aren't you. Your mind
can become agitated or unhappy; but it is not you.

Thus as you become centered you become less vulnerable, less easily hurt. This brings a sense of
peace. As you become centered you find a clear, calm
witness of yourself. This witness is at peace and
thus brings peace. So becoming centered and learning
to stay centered leads to an inner peace that fills
your being.

Becoming centered is a gradual process that usually involves small steps and subtle changes. At first
you may only be centered occasionally, such as when
things are going well in your life, when you are in a
very peaceful mood, or during some meditation. However,
most of the time you are not centered, and some of the
time, as when you are angry or anxious, you are not
able to be centered. With some work and experience
you will learn to be centered more and more. Now an
inner peace will gradually grow within you. So the
process continues on and on as your inner peace grows
stronger and deeper. Eventually you will be quite
centered much of the time and this will greatly improve your life.

The way one becomes more and more centered is
discussed next. It involves quieting your mind,
opening your heart, cultivating unconditional acceptance, and going with the flow.

QUIETING YOUR MIND
Most people's minds are continually running all
day. A typical mind goes think, think, remember, perceive, react, think, perceive, think, plan, remember,
remember, perceive, think, think, and so on at a fast
rate. Now with this going on all the time the average
person spends most of his or her life lost in thought.
You will have trouble becoming centered if you are
dominated by the activity of your mind. Thus it is

important to learn to quiet your mind.

Quieting your mind means slowing it down and learning to focus and hold it on what you choose. It involves working with your mind so you control it rather than it controlling you. This will make your mind more effective and improve your thinking and creativity.

The best way for most people to quiet their minds is through meditation. How to meditate is described in Chapter 6 (Relaxing Body and Mind). You might wish to review that section now and begin meditation if you have not done so yet. Further meditation instruction is given in the next chapter.

Another thing you can do to quiet your mind is to decrease the great amount of evaluating you do. Decrease judging yourself and others. Decrease rating things. Decrease having opinions about so much. Decrease categorizing and labeling everything.

There are times when you need to evaluate. But most people do much more evaluating than is necessary. So decreasing evaluating quiets the mind.

OPENING YOUR HEART
Opening your heart means to develop compassion, concern, and unconditional acceptance for yourself, other people, animals, plants and everything else. Opening your heart means loving more, as discussed in the last chapter. One of the best ways of opening your heart is learning to forgive more, others and yourself. Don't hold bad feelings or resentments. Forgive, let go of these destructive feelings and thoughts, and love unconditionally. Opening your heart helps you become more centered and becoming more centered helps you open your heart. Quieting your mind and opening your heart are two of the most important things you can do for your personal, conscious, or spiritual growth.

UNCONDITIONAL ACCEPTANCE
From your work with the previous two chapters you already have some understanding of unconditional acceptance and how it might be developed. Further work with unconditional acceptance will help you become more centered and will lead to an inner peace which will enrich your whole life.

To review, there are three aspects to how unconditional acceptance fits into your life: (1) In every
situation do whatever you believe is the appropriate
and right thing to do. This may involve trying to
change situations and/or how people think and act. Be
content if you have done your best, regardless of outcome. (2) Don't needlessly worry over things you can't
change. This useless worry impairs your thinking,
causes unhappiness, and keeps you from being centered.
If you are religious, you might take these things you
can't change and turn them over to God. Then knowing
the problem is in the best possible hands you can turn
your attention to other things. (3) Before, during,
and after you have done the first two steps, unconditionally accept reality as it is. Do not upset yourself because reality is not how you want it to be or
believe it should be. Do not distort your perception
of reality to suit your needs and beliefs. See reality
as it is. Always be totally honest with yourself about
all of this.

It is all right to have preferences and try to
achieve them (step 1). But it is a mistake to get
upset if your preferences are not fulfilled (step 3).
For example, it is good for you to work hard for a
political or social cause you consider important. But
it is bad for you if you make yourself mad or depressed
when things don't go the way you want.

Developing unconditional acceptance will lead you
to a sense of freedom in which you are happy if something happens and can be equally happy if it doesn't
happen. This freedom from the events of the world
removes heavy burdens from your life and clears the
way for you to settle into a very free inner peace.

It is true for everybody that in the game of life
you win some and you lose some. Most people are happy
when they win and sad when they lose. The sadness is
unnecessary. They are sad because they want to be
winning rather than losing and/or feel they should be
winning. You don't have to do this to yourself. When
you are losing, recognize that you win some and lose
some and here is one you are losing. Unconditionally
accept that and don't make yourself upset. Alter the
situation, avoid making the same mistake again, or
whatever is appropriate for you to do. But don't make
yourself upset.

A sense of humor is very useful in developing un-

conditional acceptance. Have fun living your life.
Laugh at yourself and the traps you fall into. Be
amused when the world suddenly gives you something unexpected. Try to do what is best and right, but don't
take everything too seriously. Have a good time and
go with the flow.

GOING WITH THE FLOW

Imagine everyone swimming in the river of life.
Most people are fighting against the currents or trying to swim upstream. At the same time they are com-
plaining the river isn't going in the right direction.
Also most of the people don't know the river very well
so they run into stones and branches, which they argue
should not be there.

Now as you become more accepting and centered you
get to know the river better and thus you run into
fewer obstacles. As you get to know yourself better
and improve yourself, as with this book, you become
a better swimmer in the river of life. You are better
able to swim around in the river and better able to
control your own destiny. Meanwhile some others are
hanging onto rocks and crying about where they are.

As you become more accepting and centered you more
easily ride with the currents of the river, rather than
fighting against them. This way you travel where you
want faster, easier, and much more pleasantly.

Finally, all this leads to knowing the river well
and your part in it. At this point you can effectively
alter the course of the river itself.

Going with the flow involves not fighting life.
It requires being aware of the currents of life: interests and concerns of others, personal and professional responsibilities, social pressures, economic
limitations, to name only a few. Going with the flow
involves riding with such currents and helping to
redirect them.

Going with the flow involves more emphasis on
being than doing. Don't just try to do the honest
thing, try to be an honest person. Stop seeking happiness and start being happy. Don't divide your life
into work and play; work at changing your mind so it
is all play.

As you go with the flow you stop fighting life.
As you stop fighting life you become more centered.

BEING CENTERED
     After doing the things described in this chapter,
there will be times when you feel centered and times
when you won't. Gradually you will learn to notice
many differences between being centered and not, differences in the way you feel, think, and perceive. You
will notice differences in your relaxation, compassion,
ability to love and accept, and sense of inner calm.
Noticing these differences will help you stay centered
more often and become even more centered.

     When you notice you are being pulled off center,
this is an important opportunity to improve your life.
Look for what is pulling you off center. It might be
an emotion, such as anger or anxiety. It might be a
desire, such as a sexual desire or a craving for a
drug. It might be that you are running a model of
yourself or the world against reality. Or it could
be one of many other things. See what it is. Make a
list of the things that pull you off center. Then do
something about them, as with the techniques of this
book. As you learn to keep things from pulling you
off center, you will find it easier and easier to
stay centered.

     Remember all of this is a gradual process. Don't
be impatient. Take small steps. Take on what you can
and let the rest go. Do your best. Try to continually
progress. Then totally accept yourself exactly where
you are -- unconditional acceptance.

     As you become more and more centered more and more
of the time, there will gradually arise a sense of
inner peace. This peace is so powerful you will consider it one of the best gifts you have ever received.
And you have it all inside now. All you need to do is
clear away some obstacles and let it be.

CHAPTER TWENTY-SIX

MINDFULNESS

In this chapter you will learn to expand your mind and become more aware. You will learn to notice things you overlooked before. You will find beauty in things you took for granted. This increased awareness is called mindfulness.

This whole book is intended to help you know yourself better. You have been learning to objectively observe the way you act, feel, and think. You have been learning to notice the various cues that influence you, such as situations that make you feel anxious or happy. You have been learning how your thoughts and feelings affect each other. You have been becoming more mindful of your life. This chapter shows you how to greatly increase this mindfulness you have begun. The best place for most people to begin is with meditation; however, if meditation does not suit you right now, skip this section and move on to the exercises in the rest of the chapter.

MEDITATION

For many people meditation is the most powerful tool for becoming more mindful. The more experienced you are with meditation, the more you will profit from this chapter. If you have never practiced meditation or have not meditated for a while, read the section on meditation in Chapter 6 (Relaxing Body and Mind). Practice meditation as described there for a few weeks before continuing with the rest of this section!

Assuming you have been meditating for a while, here are further meditation instructions:

Relax. Meditation is a time for relaxing body and mind. You should relax before beginning meditation and then stay relaxed. While meditating practice being aware of how relaxed you are. Be aware of how your body feels and how much your mind races about. Do not think about these things, just notice them. Cultivate a sense of relaxed, detached observation.

Be open. While meditating, develop an attitude of openness. Be ready for new experiences without deciding in advance what they must be. Be open to new understandings and insights without resisting what you may learn. Be willing to learn more and more about yourself. There is no threat here. Everything is okay. Relax and be open.

Make friends with yourself. Meditation is a time just to sit and be with yourself, unconditionally accepting yourself as you are. Be totally accepting of yourself no matter what happens. Whether you believe meditation is going well or poorly, make friends with yourself and accept the way the meditation currently is. If you discover something about yourself that you don't like, don't dislike yourself. Accept yourself as you are, make friends with yourself, and then change whatever you decide to change. During meditation be aware of anything you think or feel that is negative about you. Just notice it and then make friends with yourself. If you can't accept yourself when you are just sitting still, what happens when your life is more complex? Relax, be open,and make friends with yourself.

Have no goals while meditating. You should not be trying to accomplish or achieve anything while meditating. It is a time just to sit and be aware. Quiet your mind, get centered, relax, and just be. Don't have goals for what should happen, just be aware of what does happen, without an attitude of gaining or accomplishing anything. You may have reasons for meditating, things you expect from it. Great. But when meditating, just do it; don't expect or demand anything. If expectations or thoughts of accomplishment arise during meditation, just notice them but don't get lost in them. If not having any goals while meditating makes you feel you are wasting time, just notice these thoughts and feelings and "waste" some time.

Be here now. Meditation is a time to be in the here and now. It is not a time to be lost in memories of the past or thoughts about the future. Be aware of what is going on right now. Be aware of your body, your breathing, and how relaxed you are. Don't get lost in daydreaming and fantasies. Be aware of your feelings and thoughts as they are now. Don't get lost in the past or future. If memories of the past arise, notice them and return to the here and now. If plans or expectations for the future arise, notice them and return to the here and now. Realize there is only the here and now. The past is gone; memories are just mental activity in the present. The future is imaginary; plans and anticipations are just mental activity in the present. Be aware of all your mental activity.

206

But be aware from the here and now.

Be mindful. Meditation is an ideal time to practice mindfulness. Just sit and be aware. Notice all
feelings, thoughts, and intentions. Just notice. Don't
think about what you notice, just notice. Continue to
keep your attention gently focused on your point of
meditation, such as your breathing. Then any time any
thought or sensation arises, notice it and gently, but
firmly, return your attention to your breathing.

A good way to improve your noticing and mindfulness is to name what you notice. If you are watching
your breathing by the rising and falling of your diaphragm, then say "rising" to yourself when it rises
and "falling" when it falls. Or if you are watching
your breathing some other way, say "in" when you inhale
and "out" when you exhale. Now during meditation when
you start thinking about something, notice what you
are doing, say "thinking" to yourself, and return your
attention to your breath. When visual images occur,
notice them and name the process "seeing," and return
to your breath. When you hear something, say "hearing"
to yourself and return to your breath. Do the same
with everything, including "feeling," "smelling," and
"tasting." When you have to move, notice the sensations of movement while you label them "moving" or
"feeling." You can use whatever labels you like. In
some cases you may want to be more specific. Thus
instead of just "thinking" you may also wish to use
the label "planning" or "remembering."

A person who is meditating on the in and out of
his breath might have a period of meditation that goes
like this: in, out, in, out, in, thinking, thinking,
in, out, thinking, out, in,out, hearing, hearing,
thinking, thinking, hearing, in, out, in, out, in, out,
in, out, in, out, feeling, feeling, thinking, in, out,
in, out, moving, feeling, thinking, feeling, in, out,
in, out....

Spend part of your meditation period each time doing this naming exercise. It will help you become more
aware and mindful. Continue to do this until you naturally notice all these things without needing to label
them.

GENERAL MINDFULNESS
As you can tell from the above discussion, developing mindfulness is practicing being more and more aware.

It is learning to be more aware of your body and your mind, more aware of your feelings, perceptions, and thoughts. As you become more mindful, you will become aware of things at a much finer and more subtle level. You will hear, see, and feel things you never noticed before. You will perceive things in greater detail and complexity. You will find great beauty in "simple" things. You will come to know yourself much better. You will better learn how your mind works. You will gain much more control over your behavior, feelings, and thoughts.

There are three ways to develop greater mindfulness: mindfulness in meditation (discussed above), mindfulness exercises, and continual mindfulness. Mindfulness exercises are specific practices that develop mindfulness in some specific area, such as mindfulness of hearing, mindfulness of walking, and mindfulness of eating. This chapter contains a number of such exercises. After you have done a number of these exercises, you can begin developing your own exercises. This can be a lot of fun and mind-expanding at the same time.

Continual mindfulness refers to the fact that no matter where you are or what you are doing it is an opportunity to become more mindful, more aware. The rest of this chapter shows you how gradually to develop continual mindfulness.

Learning to be more mindful is learning to be more aware, more conscious. It is developing your ability to observe more objectively. It is not thinking, judging, or evaluating. It is just observing. If you choose to think or evaluate, fine. But that is thinking and evaluating, not mindfulness. Mindfulness would include observing the thinking and evaluating. Mindfulness is not reacting, elaborating, remembering, or planning. Mindfulness is just noticing, including noticing any reactions, thoughts, memories, or plans.

It is very important that you remember, and perhaps review, all of this when doing the exercises that come later. Also when doing the exercises, try to perceive as if you had never perceived before. When doing a walking exercise, try to experience walking as if you had never walked before. When doing a seeing exercise, try to see as if you had just been given vision.

You will probably enjoy the various mindfulness

exercises. And if you pursue mindfulness practices, you will profit in many ways. However, like meditation, mindfulness practices are not for everyone. If anything in this chapter is too upsetting to you, stop doing it until you consult a professional counselor and/or mindfulness instructor.

MINDFULNESS OF BEHAVIOR

Practice being aware of what you do and why you do it. Be aware of how you act and what you say in different situations. What was it about that situation that caused you to act that particular way? How do others react to what you say and do? What feelings and thoughts go along with how you behave? Be more aware of your behavior. This whole book is concerned with mindfulness of behavior. You might reread some chapters of importance to you and think about how to become more mindful of that type of behavior.

MINDFULNESS OF BODY

Spend some time each day tuning into the feelings and sensations from different parts of your body. Get more in touch with your body. You might review the beginning of Chapter 13 (Nutrition and Exercise). When you feel fatigued, tune into exactly how your body feels. Notice in detail what it feels like to be fatigued. Do the same when you feel energetic, sleepy or awake, hot or cold, and anything else.

If you experience some pain or discomfort, you may wish to reduce it in some way. But in addition, practice mindfulness. Exactly where do you feel the pain? Exactly what does it feel like? See if you can put your consciousness right into the middle of the pain and explore it. Don't judge or evaluate the pain, just notice it in detail. Don't get upset because you think pain is bad and/or you wish you didn't have any pain. Just be mindful of the pain. If you get very good at mindfulness of pain, you may find it will help reduce pain and/or make it less unpleasant.

Practice being aware of the various feelings in your body when you start to feel stress, anxiety, anger, and other emotions. The greater your mindfulness here the more choice you will have over your emotions. Review Chapter 7 (Calm and Relaxed Living).

Be more aware of your breathing. You have learned to watch it during meditation. Now also during the day periodically put your attention on your breathing.

How are you breathing? Is it shallow or deep? Is it
blocked in any way, such as in one side of your nose?
Is it primarily chest breathing or diaphragm breathing?

Practice being aware of the various sensations of
movement. Exactly how does it feel when you move some
part of your body? Try to feel this in detail.

EXERCISE 1: SIMPLE MOVEMENT. Sit down and relax.
Quiet your mind for a few minutes. Sit still. Now
slowly move one of your fingers. Move it in different
ways and different directions. Put your full attention
on the feelings of movement. Feel the movement as if
you have never felt movement before. How does it feel
when you will your finger to move? What is this feeling of willing? What part of you is doing this willing?

Over time come back and do this exercise many
times. In place of your finger use various parts of
your body to move, such as your arm, leg, or tongue.

EXERCISE 2: WALKING. Relax and quiet your mind.
Now walk very slowly. Notice in detail all the feelings
in different parts of your body as you move. Keep
your attention on these feelings of movement. Note
how each step involves lifting a leg, moving it forward,
and placing it down. Notice these different types of
movement in detail. To help you notice and hold your
attention say to yourself "lifting," "moving," and
"placing" when doing each of these.

This is a good exercise to use before and/or after
sitting in meditation. It helps bring meditation into
other parts of your life. A variation of the exercise
is to walk at a normal rate and pay attention to the
feelings of movement. You might say "right" and "left"
to yourself as you move your legs. This exercise you
can do at many times during the day when you are walking.

MINDFULNESS OF PERCEPTIONS
Every now and then stop what you are doing, quiet
your mind, and put all your attention on one of your
senses (seeing, hearing, feeling, tasting, smelling).
Notice in detail all the sensations and perceptions of
this sense. Experience the sense as if you had never
had that sense before. For example, notice the sensations of feeling as if you had never felt anything
before. Explore some object with your sense and observe the perceptions that result. For example, if

working with vision, pick something to look at and then be very aware of the various perceptions that arise as you visually explore the object.

EXERCISE 3: HEARING. Focus your attention on hearing and try to hear as if you have never heard any-thing before. Where do you feel that the hearing is taking place? Is it in your ears? Is it in the center of your head? Where do you experience hearing? Who or what part of you is doing the hearing? What is your experience of that part of you which is doing the hear-ing?

Do this same exercise with all of your other senses.

EXERCISE 4: EATING. Eat a full meal with all your attention on eating. Do not do other things such as talking, reading, or excessive thinking. Eat slowly. Experience eating as if you have never eaten before. Slowly look at the food and smell it. Slowly see, smell, and feel the food as you put it in your mouth. Feel the food in your mouth. Feel the biting, chewing, moving food around, and swallowing. Eat slowly. Notice all the different tastes and how they change.

Do this exercise every now and then. In addition, try to do something like this exercise during part of every meal. That is, try generally to become more mind-ful of your eating. You will find it will help you en-joy eating more. And if you are trying to eat less, it will help you have more pleasure with less food.

EXERCISE 5: THE WORLD. Spend one day perceiving the world as if you had never experienced any of it before. Perceive the world as if you have just arrived from another very different world. See, hear, and feel things anew, while minimizing memories you have of these things.

MINDFULNESS OF FEELINGS

Practice being more aware of your feelings. When you are feeling something you like, notice the feeling in detail and say to yourself "pleasure." When you feel something unpleasant, notice the feeling in detail and tell yourself "unpleasant" or "pain." Try to notice all feelings as soon as they arise. Then notice how the feeling changes in time and how it goes away. Just notice, don't evaluate or hang on to the feeling. Just be aware.

MINDFULNESS OF MIND

Becoming more mindful of your mind includes practicing being more aware of the contents of your mind, including thoughts, memories, perceptions, and fantasies. Spend some time each day just noticing the contents of your mind. This does not mean thinking about the contents, for that is just more thinking. Just notice the thinking, don't think about thinking. Only the mind thinks; and here you want just to observe your mind. Meditation is a good way to learn to observe your mind.

Be more aware of the general state of your mind. Is it relaxed or agitated? Is it functioning accurately or is it caught in delusions? Experience how the state of your mind relates to the state of your body.

Try to be more aware of intentions that arise in your mind. Usually before you act in some way an intention for that act arises in your mind. Most people are unaware of these intentions, so their behavior is pretty automatic. As you become more aware of the intentions that arise in your mind, you will have greater control over your behavior. You will do fewer things that you later regret.

Review Chapter 11 (What Do You Think) and practice mindfulness for the things discussed. For example, practice noticing what you say to yourself in different situations and when you are being negative and/or irrational.

Review Chapters 23, 24, and 25 (Happiness, Love, Inner Peace) and practice mindfulness for what is discussed. For example, be more aware of when you fall into the "more is never enough" trap. Be more aware of when you are making yourself unhappy because reality does not match your idea of how it should be. Be more aware of how accepting you are of people and situations. Realize that becoming more mindful of your thoughts will help you become more thoughtful.

EXERCISE 6: VISUALIZING. Close your eyes and visualize an object you know well. Visualize it in as much detail as possible. Observe your mental processes as images form in your mind. Where do you feel that this visualizing is taking place? Who or what part of you is observing these visualizations?

Do this exercise with many different objects to

visualize. Then move into more complex things such as
people you know. Be aware of any feelings or thoughts
that arise during visualizing.

EXERCISE 7 : THINKING. Close your eyes, quiet
your mind, and then think about something. Observe
your thoughts as if you have never encountered thoughts
before. Do not think about your thoughts, just notice
them. Where do you feel this thinking is taking place?
Who or what part of you is observing these thoughts?
What is the difference between you and your mind?

Do this exercise many times, thinking about different things. Start by thinking about fairly simple
things and move toward thinking about things for which
you have strong feelings. Notice differences in the
way that you think and how well you think that are
caused by what you are thinking about.

THE WITNESS
As you develop mindfulness you are developing a
witness to yourself. The witness is a silent observer
of everything. The witness does not feel; it just
observes feeling. The witness does not think, evaluate,
decide, or will. These are all functions of the mind.
The witness just observes. Whatever arises in your
consciousness is noticed by the witness.

The witness lives in a very quiet, peaceful, centered place. The witness is not vulnerable. Nothing
can hurt the witness. The witness does not feel unhappy; it just notices unhappy feelings.

Opening yourself to the witness in you provides
you a vantage point which is clear, objective, and
free. When you start to get upset, the witness
notices "getting upset." This gives you more understanding and control of yourself at the time. When
you are mentally criticizing someone else, the witness
notices "criticizing." This helps you cut down on
this destructive activity.

EXERCISE 8 : THE WITNESS. Who or what part of
you is this witness? How do you experience the witness? Where do you experience the witness? Who or
what part of you is experiencing or observing the
witness? Who are you? What is the real nature of
your being?

This is a very difficult exercise that you might

213

try every now and then. The "answers" to the questions
of the exercise are not intellectual answers; they are
answers that come from direct experience. That is, the
questions are concerned with total experiences, not
your thoughts. Also the "answers" to the questions
will probably continually change as you practice the
exercise and go deeper into your being.

BE MINDFUL
    The essence of this chapter is to just be more
aware of your behavior, body, perceptions, feelings,
and mind. It is a matter of intentionally working at
being more aware, more conscious. With practice over
time it will become easier and easier and soon will
be quite natural and automatic. As you become more
mindful you will be amazed and delighted at what you
will discover. And it will lead you to levels of understanding and freedom beyond what you can currently
imagine.

SUGGESTED READING

    The Cook and Davitz book is a collection of ex-
ercises including mindfulness exercises and visualizing.
The exercises are designed to require from 60 seconds
up to 20 minutes. The best mindfulness material is
found within the Buddhist literature, particularly the
Theravada Buddhist practices. You can easily practice
Buddhist mindfulness without getting involved in any
particular philosophy or religion. Dhiravamsa has
issued an excellent, readable, and useful book on
Buddhist mindfulness. Goldstein offers instruction
in meditation and mindfulness from a Buddhist orientation. Kornfield had compiled the mindfulness instructions from a variety of different Buddhist teachers.
For the person who wishes to pursue meditation in
greater detail, Suzuki's book is superb.

Cook, H. & Davitz, J. 60 seconds to mind expansion.
    Random House, 1975. Pocket Books paperback, 1976.
Dhiravamsa, V. R. The way of non-attachment.
    Schocken, 1977.
Goldstein, J. The experience of insight: A natural
    unfolding. Unity Press, 1976.
Kornfield, J. Living Buddhist masters. Unity Press,
    1977.
Suzuki, S. Zen mind, beginner's mind. Weatherhill,
    1970.

CHAPTER TWENTY-SEVEN

COMMUNICATION

Communication involves exchanging ideas, information, opinions, attitudes, and feelings. Poor communication is a major cause of problems between people,
including people who have lived together for years.
Bob misunderstands what Betty is saying and they end
up in an unnecessary argument. Susan doesn't listen
to her son's point of view and a barrier develops between them. Jack keeps many of his feelings to himself which results in his boss unknowingly giving Jack
assignments he doesn't like.

Fortunately there are many things you can do to
improve your communication. This chapter includes
some of the most important. As your communication
improves, your personal and professional relationships
will improve and your life will generally be happier
and more effective.

LISTENING

The most important communication skill is good
listening. To communicate well you must hear what the
other person thinks and feels. Even if you are primarily interested in saying something yourself or influencing the other person, you will be most effective
if you listen well, for then you will better judge
when the other person can best hear you and you will
say what you have to say in the best way. Good listening is also good manners and people generally like to
be listened to. And many times that a friend of yours
has problems the best thing you can do is to be a good
listener.

However, most people are terrible listeners. When
a person should be listening, the drunken monkey of his
or her mind is running about evaluating, reacting, and
planning what to say next. As the topic of conversation becomes more personal or controversial, the
amount of listening dramatically decreases. People in
a conversation are often competing to talk and using
most of the time others are talking to prepare what
they are going to say. Now if you only really listen
to 20 or 30 per cent of what the other person is
saying, you will probably misunderstand him, miss some
important points, and/or inappropriately react to something out of context.

215

So it is important to practice listening to other people. Quiet your mind and listen. Keep your mind from wandering about and listen. Don't judge or evaluate; just listen. You can evaluate later if you wish, after you have listened and understood. Don't plan what you are going to say next; just listen. You will do a better job of talking if you listen than if you plan replies. Also you can always stop and think about what you will say. It is not necessary for someone always to be talking, even in a conversation. Quiet your mind and listen. If you notice that you are interrupting others, you probably are not listening. Meditation may help you learn to quiet your mind (see Chapter 6, Relaxing Body and Mind).

Listen to the facts, ideas, and opinions of the other person. Listen carefully for the feelings that the person has for what he is saying. Listen for how feelings are reflected in the person's emphasis, inflections, loudness of voice, and choice of words. Listen carefully; there is much more to hear than you usually hear. Listen with your eyes as well as your ears, for a person communicates many of his thoughts and feelings by facial expression, hand gestures, and body position. There is so much going on you need to listen very carefully. All of this is also an excellent exercise in mindfulness, the topic of the last chapter.

While listening, try as best you can to see, think, and feel from the other person's point of view. If you have trouble with this, you might try the role reversal strategy discussed at the end of Chapter 12 (Mental Rehearsal).

Let the other person know you are listening. Nod or shake your head when appropriate. Make brief comments such as "That was unfortunate" or "That is really interesting." Ask questions. Show you are listening, interested, and concerned.

HONESTY

Learning to be honest with yourself has been a theme throughout this book. It is to your advantage to see yourself as you really are and not to fool yourself. Learning to be honest with others will make life more easy, improve communication, and make you most helpful to others. The importance of honesty has been stressed by teachers and philosophers for thousands of years. Honesty is a fundamental part of all the major world religions.

Yet just about everyone is dishonest with others some of the time. A husband, trying to be nice, tells his wife he likes her new dress when he really doesn't. An alcoholic avoids needed professional help because he is too embarrassed to admit he has a drinking problem. A doctor tells a patient he is getting better when the doctor really knows he is dying. All of this dishonesty is destructive. The wife ends up with a dress she believes pleases her husband. If he had told her the truth she might have exchanged it for a dress they both like. Instead she has a dress he doesn't like, which probably affects his mood. All of this is very unfair to her. The alcoholic avoids needed counseling and his life continually gets more problematical. The doctor deprives her patient of a very important right, the right and need to prepare for one's own death. There may be many practical, legal, family, psychological, and spiritual things the patient would want to do and/or should do.

Being honest does not mean having no judgement or tact. You may not like the anchovy-applesauce salad at a dinner party; but there is no need to voluntarily mention this. If asked by the host, you can say you preferred the main course to the salad. If pushed on your opinion of the salad, you can say it doesn't match your taste. Your honesty may keep the host from serving you that salad in the future and/or from serving a generally unpopular salad at future parties.

Being honest doesn't mean unloading everything you think and feel about a topic. If the neighbors with unruly children ask you your opinion about their childrearing, don't give them a list of 30 things you think they are doing wrong. If it is appropriate for you to say anything, then just mention a couple of helpful suggestions. Similarly, in your relationship with someone don't store up a bunch of complaints and then dump them all out when you are angry and can't hold any more. Rather, bring up your concerns individually over time in a loving and problem-solving manner.

Being honest is saying what you mean and meaning what you say. Being honest is communicating truthfully. Thus if what you say is literally true but it leads the other person to believe something false, then you are being dishonest. Carol asked Chuck if he had problems

217

with the children at the doctor's office. Chuck said
no. Now in fact Chuck had had a lot of problems with
one of the children, but didn't want Carol to know.
So when she asked about problems with the children,
he said no since there were problems with only one
child. Now Chuck may believe he was being honest, but
he wasn't. It is what you communicate; and he commu-
nicated no problems with any of the children.

As you become more honest with others it will encourage them to be more honest with you. And all of
this will make your dealings with others simpler and
more effective.

I VERSUS YOU MESSAGES
Part of honesty is learning to separate your
opinions from fact and expressing this when you talk.
Thus it is better and more accurate to say "my favorite" rather than "the best," or say "the one most useful to me" rather than "the only one worthwhile."
Look for opportunities to begin your opinions with
phrases like "I believe..." or "It seems to me...."

Similarly, it is better to own up to your own
feelings rather than blaming someone else. If at the
end of a hard day your child's noise is bothering you,
it is better to say "I am tired and bothered by noise"
rather than "You are a pest." This is an example of
the difference between an I-message and a you-message.
It is generally better to use I-messages than you-
messages, particularly with children.

Say a friend is very late and you are angry.
Your friend is responsible for being late; but you are
responsible for being angry. Thus instead of saying
"You made me angry..." it is better to say "I feel
angry because I wanted to be on time." If your spouse
forgets your anniversary and you feel hurt, it is better to say "I feel hurt because I enjoy celebrating
our anniversary." rather than "You are inconsiderate."

Now the differences between I-statements and you-
statements may not seem like too much at first glance,
but learning to use more I-statements has many advantages: Use of I-statements encourages more problem-
solving and less assigning blame. Use of I-statements
will make you more positive toward others and will
elicit less resistance, anger, and anxiety. Your use
of I-statements helps others use more I-statements.
And all of this promotes better communication and more

218

honesty and openness.

PROBLEM-SOLVING
People are often involved in resolving conflicts, working with disagreements, and finding solutions to interpersonal problems. Good communication is very important here. Below are some general guidelines.

Be sure you have enough time. Don't try to resolve conflicts a piece at a time stuck in between other things. Create the necessary time. If the time does not seem to come by itself, then schedule the time. Many marriages are not as good as they could be because the couple does not create enough time to discuss important issues.

Stick to one issue at a time. Don't jump from one topic to another.

Put the emphasis on problem-solving, not assigning blame or matching complaint with complaint. The question is what to do now, not what was done in the past. What are you going to do now? When problem-solving, emphasize the sharing of ideas, not giving advice. Be positive: Say what you would like, not what you don't like. Say what you can do, not what you can't do.

Provide specific examples, rather than just generalities. The generality "You are self-centered" is attacking and not useful. While the specific example "You didn't ask my opinion about when we should vacation" could be more useful. When discussing examples, talk about what you observed, not what you think it means. Using I-messages, describe your own feelings and reactions; don't get caught in evaluating, criticizing, and blaming.

And while all this is going on be as mindful as possible of all your feelings, reactions, and thoughts.

Learning to communicate better, as described in this chapter, may take a little extra effort at first. But after a while it will all be very natural, easy, simple, and direct.   And you will find it greatly improves your life.

SUGGESTED READING

The first two books contain general discussions of

219

communication and provide many useful exercises. The Goldstein book deals with a number of different personal skills including many related to communication. Gordon discusses communication with children including the use of I-messages. This should not be treated as a total approach to child rearing. Gordon has similar books for others, including teachers and business leaders.

Gottman, J., Notarius, C., Gonso, J., & Markman, H. A couple's guide to communication. Research Press, 1976.

Strayhorn, J. M. Talking it out. Research Press, 1977.

Goldstein, A. P., Sprafkin, R. P., & Gershaw, N. J. I know what's wrong but I don't know what to do about it. Prentice-Hall, 1979.

Gordon, T. Parent effectiveness training. Wyden, 1970. New American Library Paperback, 1975.

CHAPTER TWENTY-EIGHT

CHOOSING A COUNSELOR

Many people can greatly improve their lives on their own when they know what to do. Books such as this one and those in the suggested readings can often help greatly. However, in many cases people can profit from help from others, in addition to the approaches of this book. It may be useful to have someone to talk with, to sort things out and clarify goals. Or a particular problem in your life may be too difficult to handle by yourself. Or you may need the help of a specialist in some area. There are also many other reasons for seeking out help from others. Below are some general suggestions for choosing a counselor.

The best counselor for you could be a relative, friend, minister, social worker, psychiatrist, psychologist, or someone else. Your needs and interests determine the best counselor for you. Be sure to choose a person who will give honest reactions and impressions (whether good or bad) and will be supportive of you. If you decide you need professional psychological help, there are a number of ways to find who is available in your area: get recommendations from friends; see if there is a community mental health center near you; get lists of names from local psychological, psychiatric, or mental health associations; check the yellow pages of the phone book; and/or get recommendations from a nearby college from their departments of psychology, social work, and psychiatry. States vary in their licensing and certification requirements for people such as psychologists and social workers. For example, in many states anyone can be a marriage counselor or sex therapist.

In many fields, such as medicine and automobile repair, there are generalists and specialists. The generalist (such as a general practitioner in medicine) has a broad general knowledge of the field, while the specialist (such as a neurosurgeon) has more specialized and detailed knowledge in one area of the field. The same is true for counselors. For your needs a counselor with general knowledge and experience may be the best choice. But if your problem area is very specific, you should find a counselor who has specialized training and experience in that area. For example, if you have a sexual problem you want a specialist whose

221

training includes the types of approaches used by Masters and Johnson. If your problem is like those discussed in Section Three (fears, weight control, smoking, alcohol), you want a counselor with specialized training in behavior modification. If treatment of your problem clearly needs the use of drugs or hospitalization, then a medical person such as a psychiatrist is probably required. Most psychiatrists' training and approach are primarily from a medical orientation.

In most cases when you seek professional help you probably should see a psychologist. Unfortunately, within psychology there is a wide range of different therapies and approaches. Some of the approaches are useful for many (not all) people. Some of the approaches are preposterous and/or harmful. Using your common sense and some of the suggestions below, you should be able to choose what is right for you.

Don't be intimidated by the counselor because he or she has a Ph.D. or M.D.,good reputation, nice office, forceful manner, or anything else. Among counselors who have all these types of "credentials" are good counselors and bad counselors, ones that are right for you and ones that are not. The first session with a counselor is usually a period of consultation in which you both decide whether this counselor and his or her approach is right for you. This is very important. Do you agree on goals and ways to achieve them?

The counselor's approach should make sense to you. If not, ask questions. If it still does not appeal to your common sense, you may be wasting your time or being sold a questionable therapy. The ideal counselor is a good listener, gives direct answers to questions, admits limitations and errors, is flexible, makes you feel comfortable and confident, does not act superior to you, and does not treat you as being sick or defective. A good counselor may not have all these virtues, but a person with few of these is probably not a good counselor. Remember, you are paying for this person's services and you have a right to be satisfied.

Another question is how long treatment will take. Here again you must use your common sense. At the one extreme, two days of treatment is too short for most complex problems. Although some things can be learned in a weekend program, it is seldom enough in the long run. At the other extreme, therapy that involves years

222

is generally inefficient for most problems.

The key to evaluating your counseling as it progresses is whether you are learning useful skills that you can apply in your daily living. Can you point out specific ways in which your life is improving as a result of counseling? If you are just learning to talk like your counselor, that is not enough. If you are just exploring your history, that is not enough. If you are just philosophizing, that is not enough. You should be learning useful skills.

Similarly, be wary of drugs. Practitioners in the medical and psychological professions are too quick to prescribe drugs. For some people drugs can be a very important part of therapy. But drugs are seldom therapy by themselves. In most cases where drugs are used, the drug should be briefly used along with learning new skills. Then the drugs should be gradually reduced and removed.

If after a while you feel that the counseling is not going as well, as fast, or in the direction you think it should, then discuss this with your counselor. A good counselor will readily discuss these concerns with you. If you are still not satisfied, then feel free to switch to another counselor. But if you find yourself switching from counselor to counselor, you may be avoiding dealing with some of your problems. Or you may be seeking a counselor who will tell you what you want to hear, which may not be the best thing for you. Or you might be the type of person who enjoys continually being a client.

Finally, be sure to check on the counselor's fees when you first call in or at your first meeting. How much is the charge per session? How long is a session? Does the fee depend on your income? How and when do you need to pay? Will your insurance apply to any of this?

There are many good counselors available to you that can help you in many ways. You just need a little patience to find the one right for you.

FEEDBACK

Although we are at the end of this book, you are continuing on a great journey. You have the opportunity to learn more and more about yourself and to significantly change your life in ways that make you more effective personally, interpersonally, and professionally. You have the opportunity to make your life much more fulfilling. I wish you the very best and I hope that this book will be useful to you along the way.

I would appreciate _any_ comments or suggestions you have about this book: parts you found particularly useful, parts that were not clear, suggestions for additions or deletions, examples of some of the ideas or principles, how you used the book, etc. This feedback will help me evaluate the book and make improvements in future editions. Thank you.

William L. Mikulas
Faculty of Psychology
University of West Florida
Pensacola, Florida
32514-0102

TECHNICAL OVERVIEW
A technical overview of content and intent
for professionals and/or practitioners

The intent of this book is to systematically help
the reader become more aware of the breadth and inter-
relationships of his actions, feelings, and thoughts
and to learn general and specific strategies for pro-
ducing change in these areas. I draw from a number
of literatures including Western experimental psychology, popularized self-help programs, Western and
Eastern personal growth approaches, and practical suggestions relative to specific problem areas.

There are two important issues I wish to address
here: the generality of this book and the intended
audiences. Concerning generality, my intent is to
cultivate practical understanding and implementation
of a number of general strategies of living (self-
help, self-control, personal growth) that can be applied in a wide range of situations and to a number of
domains of behavior and experience. The following
are some examples: The reader is gradually encouraged
and taught to be more objectively aware of his actions,
feelings, and thoughts, how they interrelate, and how
they are influenced by environment and other people.
Greater objectivity is cultivated by approaches such
as record keeping (behavioral assessment) and developing a clearer, non-evaluative, aspect of mind. Greater
awareness is cultivated through clearer objectivity
as well as specific practices aimed at body sensations
(e.g., movement, relaxation, anxiety), emotions (e.g.,
fear, unhappiness), and thoughts (both content and
processes). Relaxation is encouraged and relaxation
practices begin with the body (e.g., breathing, muscle
relaxation) and general agitation of the mind (meditation) and then gradually move toward relaxing the way
one approaches living in general. Other general
strategies include the importance of taking small
steps (shaping, hierarchies), commitment to a plan of
action (as opposed to an attitudinal change) that often
needs to be revised, and unconditional, objective,
acceptance of oneself while simultaneously recognizing
the desirability of change.

The general strategies, such as those above,

227

weave throughout the book and manifest in various forms. There is a general progression from the more obvious and easier to discriminate domains to the more subtle. While developing these general strategies the book surveys a number of specific skills and techniques that have wide applicability. Included here are such things as stimulus change, mental rehearsal, contracting, assigning priorities, habit reversal, countering thoughts, and positive thinking. (See sections one and two.)

In section three I consider a number of common problem areas (e.g., weight control, fears, smoking) and show how the general strategies and specific skills, coupled with additional suggestions, apply to these areas. Now whole books have been written on these topics that I treat in one chapter. In this book the critical components for dealing with the problem areas have already been covered in previous chapters. So any chapter in section three only needs to integrate the previous material and add some new and specific tactics.

Thus this book is more general than most self-help books and is not in "competition" with them. On the contrary, I refer the reader to many of these more specific books for when he wants and/or needs more details or elaboration. I hope this book provides the reader with a comprehensive and interrelated guide to many of the practices and books that may be of use to him.

Finally, it has been my experience in working with individuals and groups that if a person can get hold of one or two strategies that are meaningful to him and that he can practically apply, this is often more effective than trying to get him to adopt a complex program. In this book I encourage the reader to be as comprehensive in his change approach as possible; but I am not relying on comprehensiveness as the solution.

This book is intended for three overlapping populations: (1) college students learning about psychological change processes, (2) counselors and clients, and (3) the general reader interested in improving his life.

Many college disciplines (e.g., Psychology, Education, Sociology, Social Work) deal with the processes of psychological change. A common and effective way for the student to learn about these processes is by participating in a change project, usually using himself as a subject. This book is intended to be used as a manual for such projects in courses such as General Psychology, Behavior Modification, Counseling, Educational Psychology, and Personal Adjustment. In addition, it is very clear that in counseling and therapy situations it is important to stress the development of self-control in the client (self-control, locus of control, self-efficacy). This book is one example of how this might be done.

I also intend the book to be an adjunct to counseling and therapy. It is not practical for the counselor to attempt to accomplish everything in his one-to-one meetings with the client. Thus counselors more and more rely on group work, peer counseling, community groups, and self-instructional material. I am sure there are many counseling cases in which it would be profitable to have the client read some or all of this book. I would appreciate hearing from any practitioners who use the book this way. I would also encourage and welcome any research evaluating the effectiveness of the book with various subjects in various situations.

Finally, the book is intended for the average person whose interests and background make this book appropriate in content and level. A large number of people wish to improve their lives without necessarily seeking professional help. This book is a practical guide for these people.